MELVILLE

MANIFESTOS

M00022324 7

THE SCHREIBER THEORY

DAVID KIPEN

THE SCHREIBER THEORY

A RADICAL REWRITE OF AMERICAN FILM HISTORY

MELVILLE HOUSE PUBLISHING
HOBOKEN, NEW JERSEY

©2006 DAVID KIPEN

ALL RIGHTS RESERVED. NO PORTION OF THIS BOOK MAY
BE REPRODUCED—MECHANICALLY, ELECTRONICALLY, OR
BY ANY OTHER MEANS, INCLUDING PHOTOCOPYING—
WITHOUT PRIOR WRITTEN PERMISSION OF THE PUBLISHER.

BOOK DESIGN: DAVID KONOPKA

MELVILLE HOUSE PUBLISHING
300 OBSERVER HIGHWAY
THIRD FLOOR
HOBOKEN, NJ 07030

FIRST MELVILLE HOUSE PRINTING
ISBN 10: 0-9766583-3-X
ISBN-13: 978-0-9766583-3-7

PORTIONS OF THIS BOOK HAVE APPEARED, IN SOMEWHAT
DIFFERENT FORM, IN *THE SAN FRANCISCO CHRONICLE*,
THE *WORLD POLICY JOURNAL,* AND *THE ATLANTIC
MONTHLY.*

LIBRARY OF CONGRESS CATALOGING-IN-PUBLICATION DATA

KIPEN, DAVID.
 THE SCHREIBER THEORY : A RADICAL REWRITE OF AMERICAN FILM HISTORY / DAVID
KIPEN.
    P. CM. -- (MELVILLE MANIFESTOS)
 ISBN-13: 978-0-9766583-3-7
 ISBN-10: 0-9766583-3-X
 1. MOTION PICTURE AUTHORSHIP--UNITED STATES. 2. SCREENWRITERS--UNITED
STATES--CREDITS. 3. MOTION PICTURES--UNITED STATES--HISTORY. I. TITLE.
II. SERIES.
 PN1996.K485 2006
 808.2'30973--DC22

                                    2005033164

PRINTED IN CANADA

CONTENTS

*This book is gratefully dedicated to Randy Newman,
Ennio Morricone, John Barry, Jerry Goldsmith,
Elmer Bernstein, Carter Burwell, John Williams,
Rachel Portman, Thomas Newman, Howard Shore,
Miklos Rosza, Bernard Herrmann, John Addison,
Maurice Jarre, Henry Mancini, Danny Elfman,
David Shire, Wojciech Kilar and all the rest,
without whose stereophonic accompaniment I could
never have written it or much of anything else.
On the off-chance I'm full of it, and screenwriters
aren't the principal authors of their films after all,
the smart money is on you guys . . . .*

*And, with love, to Vêronique de Turenne and the
memory of Dr. Charles S. Kipen—two French imports
I can live with . . . .*

THE SCHREIBER THEORY

"Finally we shall place the Sun himself at the center of the Universe. All this is suggested by the systematic procession of events and the harmony of the whole Universe, if only we face the facts, as they say, with both eyes open."

—NICOLAUS COPERNICUS

"The writer is the most important person in Hollywood, but we must never tell the sons of bitches."

—IRVING G. THALBERG

PRE-CREDIT SEQUENCE

THE MIS-SHELVED LIBRARY

Imagine a library of novels alphabetized *by editor*. Some lunatic librarian has willfully ignored all the authors' names. Instead he's scoured the acknowledgments and dedications of each volume, searching out each obligatory thank-you "to Max Perkins, without whom..." or "Bob Gottlieb, though of course all shortcomings are my own." Taped over by spine labels identifying Perkins, Gottlieb, and the rest, the names of the people who actually wrote the books have become all but unreadable.

Screwy, no? How's a reader supposed to read and evaluate the works of an author, watching themes appear and develop the way biographical critics have been doing for centuries, if somebody's scattered the writer's books all over hell and gone?

Well, substitute "screenwriters" for novelists and "directors" for book editors, and this is exactly the way we've been encouraged to think about movies ever since the advent of *auteurist* film criticism half a century ago. According to the *auteurists*, the director deserves all the glory. Derived from the French word for "author," *auteurism* has conditioned us to concentrate on the themes and motives common to a given director's filmography, all at the expense of those poor, obscure hacks who only wrote the damn pictures.

For too long, scholars, journalists and film buffs have uncritically parroted the *auteurist* party line. The book you hold in your hand—and that you're about to buy if you haven't already, *ja?*—is an attempt to put the disarranged library of American film back in order.

The aim here will not be to replace unthinking, doctrinaire *auteurism* with an equally unthinking, writer-centered theory of film. To paraphrase E.M. Forster's *Aspects of the Novel* (in which he allows, "in a sort of drooping regretful voice, 'Yes—oh, dear, yes—the novel tells a story'"), film is, oh, dear, yes, a collaborative art. We might wish matters otherwise, but there it is. No, the point is less to supplant *auteurism* than to debunk it—and occasionally, with varying degrees of intentionality, to parody its excesses.

In other words, this manifesto can work in either of two ways. One, it might hang together beautifully and topple the *auteur* theory overnight. That would certainly be nice. But just as effective would be if, by proving that an inventive enough critic can look at *anybody's* filmography and detect thematic patterns, it shows up the *auteur* theory as no more intrinsically sound than a writer-based theory—or a cinematographer-based theory, or a *gaffer*-based theory. If we're right, of course, we win. But even if we're merely tenable, *auteurism* collapses just the same. And once that happens, maybe we can finally stop mis-shelving our movies.

DAVID KIPEN
PARADISE COVE—CAPITOL HILL

I.

ESTABLISHING SHOT

To enter a parallel universe, just dial (323) 782-4591. A blithe female voice speaks the titles of half a dozen or so current movies, the dates and times they will screen at a certain private auditorium in Beverly Hills and, finally, the names of the film-makers responsible. The titles are largely familiar. The names, to any but the most uncommon cinephile, are not. In recent years, the recording might have alerted callers to showtimes for Robert Rodat's *Saving Private Ryan*, say, or Frederic Raphael's *Eyes Wide Shut*.

Hasn't there been some mistake? Didn't Spielberg direct *Private Ryan*? Didn't Kubrick direct *Eyes Wide Shut*?

Yes, as a matter of fact, they did. They just didn't write them. And to the Writer's Guild of

America and its Film Society, whose number you've just dialed—if to practically nobody else in the filmgoing world—directing isn't everything. As for whether there's been some mistake, in fact there has, and too many people have been making it for far too long. It's called the *auteur* theory.

As developed by Francois Truffaut, Jean-Luc Godard, Eric Rohmer and other mid-century French film critics who, not coincidentally, would soon become directors, the *auteur* (rhymes with "hauteur") theory would have us believe that directors are the principal authors of their films. Its adherents contend that the best directors are those whose personalities assert themselves—despite the interference of studios, producers, and other presumed philistines—recognizably from film to film.

Alfred Hitchcock, for example, belongs in what the pioneering American *auteurist* Andrew Sarris called his "pantheon" because his films betray consistent preoccupations—in Hitchcock's case, largely with themes of guilt, paranoia, mistaken identity, and treacherous blondes. John Ford, whose pictures typically explore ideas of honor, manhood and the changing face of the American West, bunks in the pantheon for similar reasons. Similarly, Howard Hawks gets the nod because of his unfailing interest in masculine camaraderie, teasing sexuality and professional pride.

Unquestionably, these men have their names on a lot of great movies, but to read the more careless *auteurists*, greatness somehow counts for less than a one-track mind. Only a wiseacre would dare suggest that the surest way into the pantheon, therefore, is to make the same picture over and over. Such stylistically consistent directors as Hitchcock, Ford, and Hawks are all titans, but is their late work any better than—or even thematically much different from—their mature early stuff? Did these directors grow, especially? Change? Did Hitchcock's 1956 *The Man Who Knew Too Much* really mark all that much of a creative leap beyond his 1934 *The Man Who Knew Too Much*?

On the other hand, John Huston never made the same movie twice. He consequently stands outside the pantheon as either a weak *auteur* or—it gets a little hazy here—no *auteur* at all. Small consolation that no director comes close to Huston for steadfast but not slavish adaptations of literature into film. That he particularly adapted so many short novels—*The Red Badge of Courage* (scripted by Albert Band and Huston himself), *The African Queen* (James Agee, Huston again, and Peter Viertel), *Wise Blood* (Benedict and Michael Fitzgerald), *The Dead* (Tony Huston)—suggests a profound understanding of a rarely remarked cinematic phenomenon: Novellas make the best movies. Huston may not be much of an *auteur*, but—between his singular regard for fine fiction and his underrated gifts as an adapter thereof—he has a niche on the *schreiberist* Acropolis as the greatest literature director ever.

The auteur theory hasn't stood unchallenged all these years. Critics came out of the woodwork to attack Sarris after the 1963 detonation of his original grenade in the spring issue of the journal *Film Culture*. Slightly fewer detractors weighed in after his expanded taxonomy of directorial gods and demigods appeared between covers in 1968 as *The American Cinema*. The redoubtable Pauline Kael—who exerted as great an influence over the breezy, visceral style of contemporary film criticism as Sarris has over its *auteurist* substance—finally slugged back at the theory in 1971 with the book-length *Raising Kane*, her argument that Orson Welles hijacked most of the glory for *Citizen Kane* from its true author: screenwriter Herman Mankiewicz. Sounding an unmistakably proto-*schreiberist* note, Kael wrote, "[N]ow that I have looked into Herman Mankiewicz's career it's apparent that he was a key linking figure in just the kind of movies (Marx Brothers comedies, Bebe Daniels comedies, W.C. Fields in *Million Dollar Legs)* my friends and I loved best."

Then, in 1975, up rode the only counterpuncher besides Kael who ever really laid a glove on the *auteurists*. That's the year Richard Corliss published his book *Talking Pictures*, which survives—in print or, more often, out of it—as film criticism's greatest untaken offramp. There, Corliss constructed his own revisionist pantheon, and peopled it with favored screenwriters who had been locked out of Sarris' earlier shrine. For example, instead of directors Josef Von Sternberg (*Underworld*), Howard Hawks (*Scarface*), and Ernst Lubitsch (*Design for Living*), he elevated Ben Hecht, the man who wrote all three pictures.

Then Corliss went looking for which themes and idiosyncrasies each screenwriter's filmography had in common. Hecht obliged with his trademark cynicism and racy vitality, Dudley Nichols (*Bringing Up Baby, Stagecoach, And Then There Were None*) with his patented claustrophobic existentialism. Norman Krasna, George Axelrod, Howard Koch and a host of other screenwriters all came in for similar respectful treatment.

Similarly, Peter Stone (*Charade, Skin Game, The Taking of Pelham One Two Three*) repaid Corliss' interest with a knack for sprightly banter, an obsession with varieties of lying, and his seeming inability to write a character who didn't have at least two pseudonyms. Remember the character of Peter Joshua/Alexander Dyle/Adam Canfield/Brian Cruikshank from *Charade*, or the hijackers in *Pelham* with their pre-*Reservoir Dogs* aliases of Mr. Blue, Mr. Green, Mr. Gray, and Mr. Brown. (This peculiarity of Stone's extended to the screenwriter himself, who also went by Pierre Marton and other, less transparent monikers.)

There was just one problem with Corliss' revolution: It didn't stick. For one thing—and he saw this one coming a mile away—there's the confounding question of credit. As Corliss noted, a writer may get screen credit for work he didn't do (as with Sidney Buchman on the Cary Grant picture *Holiday*) or go without credit for work he did (as with Buchman on another Grant classic, *The Awful Truth*). In other words, never mind who's the *auteur* of a film; it's hard enough to figure out who's the author of the screenplay.

In addition to the conundrum of misassigned credits, any screenwriter-based theory of film inevitably has to contend with the challenge of multiple credits. Really, what would you rather try to write a cogent, humanly legible paragraph about? Sydney Pollack's *Tootsie*? Or Larry Gelbart's, Barry Levinson's, Elaine May's, Don McGuire's, and Murray Schisgal's *Tootsie*?

And with this, inevitably, we come up against *auteurism's* usual trump card. How can anyone ever hope to take screenwriters seriously as the authors of their work when half the time—and, barring such occasional happy exceptions as *Tootsie*, generally the poorer half—scripts have more than one writer?

Here, where the conversation usually stops, is precisely where it should start. Any critic worth his salt ought to be able to look at a multiple-author script and tease out themes common to each of its writers in turn—just as any decent student of comedy can tell an Eric Idle sketch from a Graham Chapman sketch, even though both are credited only to "Monty Python," or just as any self-respecting rock critic can tell whether a Lennon-McCartney song really owes more to McCartney or Lennon. Collaboration doesn't preclude analysis; it compels analysis. Yet if *auteurists* ruled the world, the master producer George Martin wouldn't just be the fifth Beatle. Because he had the sole, unshared producing credit, Martin would be the only Beatle.

So, between source material and shared credits and adaptation credits and story credits and uncredited rewrites and on-set improvisation, how's anybody supposed to give credit where credit is due?

Luckily, this isn't the rhetorical question it might once have been. After assiduous research, for example, Richard Corliss apparently determined to his own satisfaction just what Buchman did and didn't write. Careful scholarship has yielded credible approximations of how the screenplays for such contested classics as *Casablanca*, *Double Indemnity*, and *Gone With the Wind* all came to be. There's no reason to suppose that a cadre of committed film students couldn't perform a similar service for much of the rest of Hollywood history. By sifting the drafts and interviewing the surviving principals and recognizing their styles—in short, by doing the kind of old-fashioned spadework that requires too much patience for most film scholars, and too much time for even the most well-meaning daily reviewers—the nut could be cracked. But it would take a hell of a lot of shoe leather, plus more book advances and tenured fellowships than there are in heaven. Until now, it's been far easier just to assign credit for a film to its director and hope for the best.*

---

* Never mind, by the way, that plenty of movies have more than one director, even if the credits don't read that way. For example, nobody talks about "King Vidor and Victor Fleming's *The Wizard of Oz*," even if that's how a more truthful accounting of credits would read. 1939 was actually a big year for multiple-director films, what with not only *The Wizard of Oz* but also Fleming and George Cukor and Sam Wood's *Gone With the Wind*. Nor have times changed much. The Directors Guild of America still makes a shrewd, disingenuous point of insisting on sole directorial credits. Because he graciously wanted to share recognition with graphic novelist Frank Miller on 2005's *Sin City*, director Robert Rodriguez wound up having to resign from his own union.

Leaving aside the problems of imprecision and multiplicity in screenwriting credits, Corliss inadvertently sabotaged *Talking Pictures* in several ways. For one thing, he invited Sarris to write the introduction. His nemesis obliged with an essay so sportingly good-natured that Corliss' manifesto wound up sounding dogmatic and inflexible by comparison. Sarris even concluded his intro by recommending *Talking Pictures* "to everyone seriously interested in film, and especially to the millions and millions of my fellow *auteurists*. We must face up to its challenge."

So, like Mark Antony, Sarris pronounced his old NYU student Corliss an honorable man. The hint was not lost on the *auteurist* establishment Corliss had attacked, who, like good Roman legionnaires, promptly buried him for it. Newspaper book editors nationwide largely assigned the book to their film critics, who reacted much the same way art critics reacted when given Tom Wolfe's *The Painted Word*: Nice try, pat on the head, all in good fun, and now back to our previously scheduled myopia.

Corliss also slighted contemporary film by reserving only half a dozen or so of the thirty-five niches in his pantheon for active screenwriters. The rest belonged to Golden Age screenwriters like Hecht and Mankiewicz. As critical practice, this was unimpeachable. Just as the dead outnumber the living, so it is with criticism about them, and rightly so. But from a tactical standpoint, omitting all but a few working scenarists proved disastrous. Without much in the way of new work coming from his mostly deceased or retired pantheon, how could Corliss hope to be proven right or wrong, or to be argued about long enough for his ideas to gain purchase on the moviegoing imagination?

By contrast, Sarris had evaluated more than a hundred directors in *The American Cinema*, many of them just starting out. He included two appendices totaling more than a hundred pages, supplying needed chronologies and credits to a generation of fledgling *auteurists* in those pre-Internet Movie Database dark ages. True, too often Sarris predicted great things for the mediocre (Franklin J. Schaffner) and mediocrity for the great (Kubrick, Peckinpah). But to an entire generation of cinephiles, no night at the movies felt complete until they'd come home and compared their own opinions with his. People admired Corliss, but they rifled Sarris, absolutely dog-eared him.

Third, Corliss was careless: He forgot to coin a catchy name for his theory. Whatever its failings as doctrine, *auteurism* represented a masterstroke of nomenclature. Suddenly, a generation of film geeks could now impress girls, and themselves, by dropping a little French into the conversation. Next to the worldly-wise *weltschmerz* of the *politique des auteurs*, Corliss' "theory of screenwriters" sounded like a homework assignment. Plainly, the title needed work.

II.

INTRODUCTION OF THE HERO

If not "a theory of screenwriters," then what? *Ecrivainism*? No, too derivative. After auteurism, to go with another French locution would be tantamount to surrender. *Screenwriterism? Scenarism*? Somehow, these lack the exotic whiff that only a foreign language can confer. But if not French, what?

Yiddish, that's what. What language could better christen a script-based theory of film criticism than the mother tongue of many of America's first screenwriters, a language as intrinsically funny as French is highfalutin'? It naturally follows that the rightful name for this new heresy can only be: "the *schreiber* theory."

Schreiber (sometimes *shrayber*) means "writer" in Yiddish. The *schreiber* theory is thus an attempt to explode the director-centric farrago of good intentions, bad faith, and tortured logic that goes by the name of *auteurism*, and to replace it with a screenwriter-centered way of thinking about film. One way to describe such a theory would be to envision the world it might create. It's a world where the audience might make decisions on what to see more on the basis of a screenwriter's track record than a director's. It's a world where screenwriters might therefore take greater care before accepting hackwork, because their reputations as well as their solvency, might be riding on the outcome. In short, it's a world where movies might even measurably improve, since the surest predictor of a picture's quality—i.e., who wrote it would finally assume its rightful place in the equation. A filmgoer seeking out pictures written by, say, Eric Roth or Charlie Kaufman won't always see a masterpiece, but he'll see fewer clunkers than he would following even a brilliant director like John Boorman, or an intelligent actor like Jeff Goldblum. It's all a matter of betting on the fastest horse, instead of the most highly touted or the prettiest.

But is it too late for the late-blooming *schreiber* theory to supplant the hardy, non-native *auteurist* spore? Not by a longshot. The *auteur* theory is shakier than ever, thanks to a combination of bad late-career movies by some hitherto-promising pantheon candidates, a lack of productivity from others, and the generalized jejune awfulness of what passes for the American cinema in an increasingly globalized market.

This last point doesn't bode much better for a screenwriter-centered movie universe than for a director-centered one. If anything, screenwriters have it even rougher in an ever more globalized Hollywood than directors do, because dialogue—while only part of what screenwriters do—is still the part that most often gets lost in translation. Hence the proliferation not only of predominantly visual drama, i.e., action films, but of predominantly visual comedy, i.e., gross-out slapstick. Even so, it's still possible to concoct a long list of active screenwriters who have more recognizable signatures, and better batting averages, than most *auteurs*. The trick, as a glance at this book's credits should prove, becomes keeping such a list to manageable proportions.

III.

FLASHBACK

Several recent acclaimed documentaries and books have reinforced the idea of the seventies as a kind of Prague Spring for the American film director. In a sense, Corliss' 1974 *Talking Pictures* came out at precisely the wrong time. *Auteurism* had by the 1970s leached from alternative weeklies like the *Village Voice* into the mainstream press, and thence into the studios themselves. Directors were getting virtual carte blanche to make whatever movies they chose. The smart directors used this power to give gifted young screenwriters like Robert Towne (*Chinatown, Shampoo*) the opportunities they deserved, or to give such underappreciated older writers as Waldo Salt (*Midnight Cowboy, Coming Home*) their first challenging assignments in years. The not so smart directors took *auteurism* at its word and went into production with little or no script at all, leading to those few glorious debacles where, for a change, the possessory credit is amply deserved. Dennis Hopper's *The Last Movie* comes to mind here. Where *Easy Rider* began with Hopper's character selling off a large amount of controlled substances, *The Last Movie* must have begun with his ingesting them—with predictably unwatchable results.

Nevertheless, the seventies, according to received wisdom, represented a halcyon era of American film. We're regularly assured that *The Wild Bunch* and *Bonnie and Clyde* inaugurated a second flowering to rival the 1930s, and mostly it's a tenable case. Two recent books, Peter Biskind's *Easy Riders, Raging Bulls* and Ryan Gilbey's *It Don't Worry Me: The Revolutionary American Films of the Seventies*, toe the party line about '70s filmmaking with dogged *auteurist* loyalty. *Cleopatra* killed the studio system, goes this thesis, and into the breach rode a generation of young directors who first rescued, and then ruined, Hollywood—or were ruined by it. Gilbey devotes each of his ten chapters to a different '70s *auteur*: Altman, Scorsese, Spielberg, and the rest.

And yet a different thesis about '70s filmmaking, one that's at least as viable as Biskind and Gilbey's, might profile none of these men. Instead, it would devote a chapter apiece to the less erratic, more thematically unified output of the men and women who merely wrote all those illustrious directors' movies for them. Rather than draw tortured *auteurist* parallels between *The Exorcist* and, say, *Cruising*, or *Deal of the Century, or The French Connection* or *Jade,* simply because William Friedkin directed them all, such a thesis might more profitably examine the career of Robert Getchell. In the '70s, Getchell received sole screen credit for both *Alice Doesn't Live Here Anymore* and *Bound for Glory.* In the years since he's written, among others, *Sweet Dreams* and *This Boy's Life.* Yet no film scholar thinks to study Getchell's career— whatever its inevitable contingencies of fortune or favor—as an organically related whole. No, they'd rather be writing monographs on "Mirror Imagery in Friedkin's *Sorcerer.*" Add to Getchell's anonymity the similar predicaments of Buck Henry, Nancy Dowd, Salt and any number of others, and it becomes apparent that the '70s, more than the decade of the director, may well have witnessed a golden age of screenwriting.

To read most director-centric film criticism, one wouldn't suspect anything of the kind. With sometime exceptions like Corliss or Kael, most

American critics buy into *auteurist* orthodoxy without a second thought, pausing only to translate academia's jargon-bound liturgy into a wafer-thin vernacular. For decades, the tacit trans-Atlantic understanding about film has gone roughly like this: America sends France movies, and France sends America theory. French movies, brilliant though they can be, tend not to make too serious a dent at American theaters, but French theory—like a proliferating nonnative plant—has driven out any domestic attempt at a poetics of American film. We take their kudzu and pretend it's caviar.

This one-sidedness all but ignores the possibility that *auteurism*, historically, works much better as a way of discussing certain French movies than most American ones. *Of course* it makes sense to look at Godard's *Breathless* or Truffaut's *The 400 Blows* as *auterist* headbirths. Their directors wrote their own scripts—although Truffaut's many early shared screenplay credits with one Marcel Moussy surely amount to what Sarris would call "Subjects for Further Study."

Without getting all bollixed up in Platonist categories of Americanism and French-ness, it's not too far-fetched to suggest that what used to make American films recognizably American was not at all how they looked, but how their screenwriters made them sound. Between all the ex-journalists and ex-playwrights, American screenwriters gave the talkie a style that valued word above image, verbal swagger over visual sweep—not *mise-en-scene*, but *persiflage*.

Nor is this priority merely a relic of the '30s and '40s. One has only to cock an ear at the byplay between Cary Grant and Audrey Hepburn in Peter Stone's script for *Charade* (1963), or Joyce Grenfell's heartbreaking admission of her husband's death in Paddy Chayefsky's *The Americanization of Emily* (1964)—that rare movie whose hero ultimately makes a choice with which the audience is welcome to disagree—to hear the voice of Hollywood film at its most thrillingly American.

IV.

ARRIVAL
OF THE
ARCH-VILLAIN

Auteurism (not unlike the *schreiber* theory) can really only be practiced in one way: A critic sees the films, looks up or compiles the filmmaker's credits, and stares at them until patterns begin to emerge. Hardly anyone ever remarks on this low-tech methodology, but there's really no other way to do it. That's how Truffaut and Bazin must've done it, that's surely how Sarris did it, and by God that's how anybody else fool enough will do it, too.

Seen from the perspective of how *auteurists* actually work, we begin to see what so many of them have against versatility. It makes their job harder. What do Huston's *The African Queen* and *The Asphalt Jungle* have in common? Stare some more. Well, what do they? Tired yet? OK, come back to that one. Now, what do Hitchcock's *The Man Who Knew Too Much* (1935), written mostly by

Charles Bennett and Emlyn Williams, and *The Man Who Knew Too Much* (1956), adapted by John Michael Hayes, have in common? Of course! They were both directed by an *auteur*.

Biographical criticism can be defined as the presumption that patterns recur when on studies works of art by the same person together rather than separately. But stare at anything long enough, including clouds and stucco ceilings, and patterns begin to emerge. First thought, best thought—especially on deadline. (In this regard, newspaper reviewing may actually be the only vestige of automatic writing since the heyday of the surrealists.)

All this low-tech pattern recognition doesn't invalidate biographical criticism in general or *auteurism* in particular, but it should certainly humble those who elevate either to the status of dogma. And lost in most discussion of bio-crit is what effect it has on those living artists it enthrones.

This goes for the *schreiber* theory, too. Say you're Ted Tally, whose recurrent Wagnerian themes won't go unnoticed in this book's credits. Hey, you say, damn if my work *isn't* marked by undercurrents of the Gotterdammerung. But what does Tally do next? Does he start sniffing around for a "Ring Cycle" adaptation to take on? Or risk throwing his pigeonholing critics a curve, and do an original about *The Twilight of the Mortals*, or *The Surprising Comeback of the Gods*?

The effect of biographical criticism on living filmmakers offers a tidy example of Heisenberg's endlessly useful Uncertainty Principle, the one that says you can't observe a phenomenon without somehow changing it. Heisenberg was originally talking about electrons, but the idea holds true for directors as well. (And if anybody ever bothered to write about screenwriters thematically, it would apply just as unmistakably to them—maybe more so.)

Hitchcock, the only one of the original pantheon directors alive and successful enough to keep working after Sarris and the *auteurists* beatified him, was never the same after he made the cut. His reputation crested around the time of *Psycho*—whereupon his previous films grew in critics' estimation retroactively—but he never directed another movie half as good. (Actually, he did. *Marnie* was half as good.) What profiteth a director if he gain immortality and lose his talent?

The evidence for the *auteur* theory as some creative kiss of death is circumstantial, to be sure. Hitchcock is hardly the only director to have experienced, after a certain age, both an increase in critical repute and a diminution of his powers. Just because a director goes downhill around the time the *auteurists* canonize him doesn't mean the two developments are connected. But, come to think of it, the great director whom the *auteurists* most famously undervalued, John Huston, also became—coincidentally?—about the only American filmmaker to keep working at a very high level right up to his final masterpiece at eighty, *The Dead*. The question therefore becomes: What if, rather than the director's perennial champion, *auteurism* more often turns out to be his embalmer? And does the schreiber theory run the same risk for screenwriters?

They should be so lucky.

v.

UPPING
THE STAKES

Today, the pervasive question "Is there an international end to this?" has dire consequences for what sort of script gets made in America. The old emphasis on voice and script has given way to an Esperanto of violence and spectacle. Many countries have consequently condemned incursions by American culture, lamenting all the film and TV bookings lost by indigenous creations. Probably they're right.

But every bit as alarming is what this tendency is doing to American film. If France makes movies for the French, and America makes movies for the world, who's left to make movies for America? Would masterpieces like *Mr. Smith Goes to Washington*, played against a background of Washington senatorial skullduggery, or *His Girl Friday*, with its muzzle-loading, too-fast-to-translate comic dialogue, even get produced nowadays? By now the American moviegoer may only dimly remember pictures like these, which used to address him not just as a customer, but as a countryman. To put it another way, the back end is now driving the train. Wouldn't it be a shame if—after all the uproar about film authorship, to say nothing of cultural imperialism and the General Agreement on Tariffs and Trade (GATT)—the only country to lose its national cinematic identity turned out to be America?

Most of the hand-wringing about American film abroad tends to follow roughly the same line: Poor Francois, wants to take Cecile to a nice French flick, but those feelthy Yankees are hogging all the screens. Well, what about Gus, who wants to see a decent American movie like the ones he grew up on, only it so happens that item isn't on the bill of fare anymore? More and more, Gus can't even seek out a good foreign film. *Underground*, winner of the Golden Palm as the best film at Cannes in 1995, has never been released commercially in the U.S. No distributor cares to pick it up.

The export-happy American film industry runs a trade deficit exactly one night a year. That's Oscar night, when the British, the Australians, and an increasing number of international screenwriters regularly wipe the floor with Hollywood. The purpose of this demographic head-counting is not to reduce a filmmaker's vision to a mere function of his nationality, but to amplify a point. The Oscar-night trade deficit shapes up as a direct consequence of the year-round trade surplus enjoyed by an American film industry driven, except for the independents, by blockbuster comic-book adaptations that will never see the inside of the Kodak Theater on Oscar night.

Original American screenplays have it even harder than adaptations. As the savvy *L.A. Times* film columnist Patrick Goldstein has noted, "In today's Hollywood, if you're talking about serious drama, the original script is almost as extinct as the woolly mammoth." Not convinced? Just con-sider the original-screenplay nominees in 2004. They were: *The Barbarian Invasions* by Denys Arcand; *Dirty Pretty Things* by Steven Knight; *Finding Nemo* by Andrew Stanton, Bob Peterson, and David Reynolds from a story by Stanton; *In America* by Jim Sheridan, Naomi Sheridan, and Kirsten Sheridan; and *Lost in Translation* by Sofia Coppola—which won.

Take away the victorious independent film (set in Japan), and the cartoon (*Nemo*, set off the coast of Australia), and we're left with a Canadian, an Englishman, and three members of the same Irish family. (Was 2004 an exception? Hardly. The winners for both years before that, Pedro Almodovar's *Talk to Her* and Julian Fellowes' *Gosford Park*, weren't American, either. The former wasn't even written in English, nor was fellow nominee *Y Tu Mamá También*.) Terrific pictures all, but they shouldn't have had the original screenplay category all to themselves. They only did so because, for the most part, American studios have gone out of the originality business.

Globalization is a complex topic that's shipwrecked savvier sailors than this one. But let's add an element that's not often heard in the debate, and that returns us to the status of the writer in this mess: a literary perspective. The earliest fictional exemplar of globalization may lurk in, of all places, *Moby Dick*. In it Ishmael refers to all shipmates as hailing "from all the isles of the sea, and all the ends of the earth." By this Melville means that Ahab's whaler has for her final voyage hired, or press-ganged, a supremely international crew. This, today, is the venue that Hollywood is writing its pictures for: movie night on the Pequod. And we all know how well that little pleasure cruise turned out.

VI.

DEATH COMES FOR THE ARCH-VILLAIN

The smartest people in Hollywood generally agree that the *auteur* theory is arrant hogwash. Unfortunately, the smartest people in Hollywood tend to be screenwriters, who have even less power than esteem, and too often less self-esteem than either. A missed opportunity came and went in 2004, when the Writers Guild (WGA) settled for a new contract that pays much more attention to compensation and healthcare than to creative issues.

This was, in fact, the rare WGA negotiation that didn't end in a protracted strike. By contrast, directors' strikes can usually be measured in hours, after which interval the studios tend to cave and give the Directors Guild (DGA) everything the writers got and more—yet another sore point in the perpetual war between the canvas chairs and the swivel chairs.

Beyond the usual monetary negotiations over residuals in DVD, foreign, cable, satellite, and even internet markets, some of the WGA contract debate usually focuses on the so-called possessory credit. This is the notorious "A film by" credit, which at best duplicates the director's credit, but at worst awards sole authorship of a film to a director-for-hire who may have had little to do with it other than to call action and cut.

Almost all directors do more, of course, but not one of them does it alone. Nevertheless, the possessory credit remains a cornerstone of the DGA contract, and naturally the writers want it out. Such writer-directors as Phil Alden Robinson (*Field of Dreams*) have even tried to set a good example by voluntarily forgoing the possessory credit, even though they seem more entitled to it than most.

Other writers' demands in strike talks typically include an end to unlimited free rewrites by a contracted writer—which some directors, producers, and studios persist in expecting almost as a kind of tech support, or conjugal right—and the privilege of attending rehearsals and locations *if the director has no objection.* Yes, the writers' role in Hollywood has come to this: He or she currently lacks the right even to accept an invitation to the soundstage, and is in essence negotiating merely for the right to be kicked out should a director countermand the invite.

The writer's enforced absence from the set accounts for those unforgivable moments in movies when an actor mispronounces words or phrases that his character would know as well as his own name. Would Kelly Preston, playing a reporter in *For Love of the Game*, ever have been allowed to refer to her "city *editor*," with the stress on the second word, rather than her "*city* editor," if the woman who wrote the line had been present to help her? This wouldn't have usurped the director's responsibility for coaching a performance. It would merely have spared Preston the ridicule she suffered at the hands of newspaper reviewers, most of whom know all too well what a city editor is.

Rather than forever begging for respect and settling for money, here are five things that might begin to tip the balance of power in Hollywood away from the *auteurs*, and back toward those *schreibers* on whose work the whole house of cards depends. They are not in most cases strike demands, but rather quixotically offered admonitions to help safeguard their own self-respect:

1. Reform the WGA's credit-awarding procedures. How is a filmgoer supposed to recognize and appreciate the

work of the finest screenwriters until movie credits more accurately reflect their labors? Under current rules, the original writer on a project can retain at least shared screen credit even after someone else has thrown out every scene and started from scratch. Conversely, script doctors can rescue a film from oblivion and get no more acknowledgment than a paycheck and a "Special Thanks" in the closing credits—tucked between the local film development commission and the director's mom. Maybe the writers themselves don't mind getting credit for other people's work, or forfeiting credit for their own, but audiences deserve the truth. In the long run, it can only redound to the prestige of the profession.

Of course, this may lead to credits forty names long if the Guild doesn't...

2. Appoint a WGA trainee, as each new film starts shooting, to research the script's evolution and monitor its realization. The trainee would have no power to protect a script, only to record its travails. Every new line or scene and its author would be recorded, ultimately resulting in a completely annotated transcript of the finished film, available online and copy-protected at the Guild's website. This way, arbitrated screen credits would keep to manageable size, but anyone interested in a detailed version could consult one. Sound like a major bookkeeping

nightmare? Not really, and not unprecedented. After all, the DGA has placed trainees on all union shoots for years. It might require some expense for the WGA to do likewise, but reward would come in the form of credits that finally reflect with accuracy who wrote what. This program would have the added benefit of showing any starry-eyed aspiring screenwriters exactly what they're in for.

As for straightening out credits on old movies...

3. Task the WGA's credit restoration committee—who spent several years putting blacklisted writers' names back on pictures they wrote behind fronts in the '50s—with researching and reapportioning credits from other decades. It would take years, but the result would be worth it. McCarthyism has nothing on Hollywood itself for scrambling writers' credits into indecipherability. Several Golden Age chestnuts have credits for 'screenplay by,' 'story by,' 'screen story by,' 'adaptation by,' ad infinitum— many awarded on the basis of little more than whom Louis B. Mayer might have gone to the track with that day.

Leaving aside the matter of credits, it's also necessary for the WGA to...

4. Sponsor, and even host, retrospectives devoted to the works of individual screenwriters. Currently, museums,

universities and the few surviving rep houses regularly screen film tributes to directors, actors, studios, genres, countries, and God knows what all—everything, it seems, but screenwriters. How are we supposed to judge fairly whether this *schreiber* theory of screenwriter-centered film criticism is viable, or as big a crock as the *auteur* theory, unless we can study and compare the works of screenwriters in the time-honored chronological festival format? (Program enough of these and maybe the AFI will finally take the hint and honor a screenwriter with its—by now sadly cheapened—Life Achievement Award. This used to honor septuagenarian directors and the occasional actor but, since its move from network television to cable, has recognized only middle-aged actors and George Lucas.)

And finally...

5. Offer a good academic press a continuing arrangement to publish the memoirs of distinguished screenwriters. The university presses of Kentucky and California—the former known for its film biographies, the latter for its indispensable "Backstory" oral history series—would probably start a modest bidding war over such a proposal. Screenwriters themselves might prove similarly eager. Most of them started out writing some form of narrative prose, and might relish the prospect of tuning up their

old chops. They could also help rebut some of their collaborators' attempts to arrogate credit over the years. The lure of the last word—a writer's answer to final cut—is never to be underestimated. Maybe even one of the film-savvier trade presses, such as Faber & Faber or Newmarket (whose utilitarian "Shooting Script" series publishes more new screenplays than anybody else going), or a non-profit like Red Hen Press might get into the act.

These five injunctions alone won't redress decades of second-class citizenship for the screenwriter, but they can only help. Producer-prince Irving Thalberg himself said it succinctly: "The writer is the most important person in Hollywood, but we must never tell the sons of bitches." The wonder of it is, the sons of bitches have always known. They just kept it to themselves, or grumbled about it only in like-minded company.

Of course, if screenwriters are finally serious about overthrowing *auteurist* rule, they can start by not climbing all over themselves—and sometimes each other—to become directors. How is anybody supposed to respect a profession that everybody's forever stampeding to get out of, or at least trying to parlay into a dual career? Plus, it doesn't often work. The WGA rolls are littered with the stunted careers of those who tried to bust out of the writers' ghetto and failed. They get into it principally to protect their scripts—"I only direct in self-defense," Mel Brooks once said—but usually one of several things happens to such would-be hyphenates: One, they fail and can't regain their footing as screenwriters. Two, they neither fail nor succeed, but merely grow old waiting for a green light—like Richard Carstone in *Bleak House*, wasting away while suing for his legacy. Three, some succeed as directors but, seduced by the prestige, happy to delegate such bothersome chores to underlings, never write again. Or four, a happy remnant succeed as writer-directors, inflame the dreams of their fellow scribes, and, like Robert Towne, maybe even get to write and direct a movie every five or six years. By contrast, undistracted by the aspiration to direct, Howard Hawks' frequent collaborator Jules Furthman—admittedly, under a more prolific system—helped write more than a hundred pictures.

In the French Resistance, of course, collaborators were shot; in Hollywood, the worst they can expect is a stab in the back. Between now and the next Hollywood labor negotiation, the backs of erstwhile collaborators—writers, directors, studios watching nervously from the sidelines—will be stabbed, scratched, and closely watched.

Logs will be rolled and chips bargained. If another work stoppage actually comes to pass, we'll all have plenty of time to catch up with old movies. Yesteryear's masterpieces should hold up to fresh scrutiny just fine. But with more and more of movie history only a Netflix queue away, will our old assumptions about movie authorship hold up even half so well?

VII.

DOLLY OUT

The philosopher James Hillman once called a book *We've Had a Hundred Years of Psychotherapy and the World's Getting Worse*. In that same spirit, any theory has to be judged not just by its internal consistency and external applicability—both tests that *auteurism* tends to flunk—but also by the world it makes. According to that yardstick, it wouldn't be out of line to note that we've had half a century of *auteurism*, and American movies are getting worse.

This is hardly all *auteurism*'s fault. *Auteurism* didn't consolidate studio ownership under international conglomerates. It's not responsible for trashing the American educational system that produces our homegrown filmmakers, or for the globalization of entertainment, or for a domestic economy with so little slack in it, so little *play*, that lately our movies need to deafen us just to catch our attention.

Nevertheless, if only as a thought experiment, it's worth trying to isolate *auteurism* from all the other factors impinging on the movies over the last half century—or at least to behave as if we could. If we do that, it becomes pretty clear that *auteurism* is anything but a harmless fiction, a directorial power grab with few practical consequences beyond the consulting rooms of screenwriters' psychiatrists. On the contrary: *Auteurism* is a myth that came true, and the movies are suffering for it.

To grasp how the *auteur* theory evolved from a simple mischaracterization of movies at mid-century to an uncomfortably accurate description of the same medium at century's end, let's take an admittedly oversimplified look at what preceded it. For roughly the first fifty years of its history, with the possible exception of the dozen years separating *Birth of a Nation* from *The Jazz Singer*, most people regarded film as not a director's but a *producer's* medium. Such mogul-producers as Mack Sennett, Louis B. Mayer, Irving Thalberg, Jack Warner, Darryl Zanuck, Sam Goldwyn, Hal B. Wallis, Harry Cohn, Walter Wanger, and David O. Selznick got most of the ink not already lavished on actors. Directors and writers had to squabble over what little attention was left.

Only with the advent of the *auteur* theory did the balance of power begin to shift. Critics and scholars went back and reshuffled the deck, locating the real creative power in the hands of directors, and ransacking their inevitably uneven filmographies for signs of thematic coherence. When this enterprise conflicted with the facts—when critics were presented with incontrovertible evidence of producers' meddling or even, *mirabile dictu*, of screenwriters' contributions to the finished product—*auteurists* devised a dodge that rivals Freud's idea of "reaction formation" for unimpeachable circularity. Just as the Freudians could explain warm feelings toward another person with equal ease either as love or repressed hate, critics could define *auteurs* either as charismatic creators who exerted remarkable control over all aspects of their films, or as beleaguered artists who had to smuggle their virtuosity past the insensitive philistines who paid them. Whichever way you played it, the house always won.

I'd argue that in no decade but the 1950s could directors have seized such an advantage. At any other time in film history, producers and writers would have fought back with every weapon at hand, fair or dirty. But producers were busy reeling from the twin onslaughts of the Supreme Court's consent decrees (which robbed the studios of their theaters) and television (which bid fair to steal their customers). Writers, meanwhile, were running scared from McCarthyism and understandably too worried about their very livelihoods to recognize the power shift taking place around them. Not that directors and producers didn't suffer under the witch-hunts too, but, just as writers were disproportionately drawn to socialism in the 1930s and '40s, so too did those writers bear the brunt of red-baiting when the worm turned.

By the 1960s and especially the '70s, as discussed in Chapter III, *auteurism* had infiltrated both the corridors of studio power and the popular press. Directors were the new princes, and for a while their hegemony resulted in some terrific movies—almost all of them from filmmakers with sense enough to recognize the importance of a good script. Only when directors started to believe their own clippings did they later rush into production with underwritten pictures, accelerating the cycle by which yesterday's *auteur* becomes tomorrow's burnout. New *auteurs* kept supplanting the old, and not until recently have any observers begun to suggest that maybe the whole model is out of whack. Could it be that, like astronomers before Copernicus, cinephiles have been looking the wrong way all along?

To recap: For half a century, then, most critics saw film primarily as a producer's medium, and the medium obliged. Whoever the personnel, an MGM picture had MGM gloss, and a Warners picture had Warners grit. When the consensus shifted over the last fifty years—concurrent with the slow-motion collapse of the studio system—suddenly nobody could tell a Warner picture from an MGM. To tell a Kubrick film from a David Lean, though, supposedly just a frame sufficed.

American film history may currently be entering its third act. If the first fifty years or so belonged to the producer, and the second fifty to the director, who knows who might inherit the next fifty? Of course, it's the contention of this book that, despite the shifting tides of critical theory, film has always been a writer's medium. But theories have a sneaky way of affecting the phenomena they purport to describe. Just as critics can't describe an individual filmmaker's career without affecting its course—there's that Heisenberg Principle again—they can't overemphasize directors or underemphasize screenwriters in general without affecting the way people think about the whole filmmaking equation.

Now the clock is running out on the age of the *auteur*, at least in America—as even some dyspeptic *auteurists* have acknowledged. There's evidence to suggest a retrenchment is under way, whereby strong if not always visionary producers like Jerry Bruckheimer and Harvey Weinstein are wresting power back from the director.

But what if the wind were to shift a different way?

It would take some serious wishful thinking to look at the current filmmaking landscape and see a terrain ripe for *schreiberist* revolution. Screenwriters are, by and large, the same well-compensated, peevish lot they've always been.

Nevertheless, as I've suggested, theories don't just describe behavior—they shape it in subtle ways. Mainstream *auteurist* criticism put a little steel in harried directors' spines, and ever-insecure studio executives started chasing after new directorial talent for fear of appearing behind the times. Emboldened by the *auteurists'* hero worship, film directors began to see themselves as artists. Their movies got a little better for it at first—and a lot worse for it later—and their agents started haggling more aggressively on their behalf. The myth of the *auteur*, once merely the wishful thinking of a few directors manqué, had finally come true.

It would be nice to find a smoking gun, some canceled check in the Directors Guild archives made out by Cecil B. DeMille to Andrew Sarris, with a memo line reading "Vast Auteurist Conspiracy— PAID," but that's not going to happen. (Might make a nice maguffin for a Hollywood thriller, though.) No, the *auteurs* have trumped the *schreibers* through a shabby confluence of directorial ego, writerly insecurity, studio favoritism and critical laziness. The success of the *auteur* theory is the product of countless collaborators—just like the good movies it purports to explain, and the bad ones it labors to explain away.

What's needed now, before the irredentist Bruckheimerian reaction consolidates its gains, is an equally powerful *schreiberist* countermyth. With this book, I hope I've begun to lay out the case for just such an antidote. I'm trying to make an argument for *schreiberism* not just as a viable competing theory, but as a necessary practical prelude to finally getting a few better movies made. In the 1970s, a few directors tried living up to the *auteurists'* overstated claims for their profession and, for a while there, it actually worked. Just imagine if screenwriters, with so much greater right to those claims, held themselves to a similar standard.

THE

END

ROLL CREDITS

THE LIVES OF THE SCREENWRITERS

From here, the focus shifts to scholarship—to the steady spadework of recovering forgotten screenwriters and rehabilitating overshadowed ones. Hives of bushytailed grad students and DVD reviewers will be needed to shoehorn back into the history books the hundreds of screenwriters airbrushed out of them for so long. What follows is the barest beginning of how such an enormous revisionist undertaking might look. The effort will be complicated by diminishing space for intelligent film reviewing in American newspapers and shrinking budgets at American publishing houses, where critical biographies of hitherto obscure screenwriters aren't exactly a priority. At the very least, a biographical dictionary of screenwriters is needed to take its place alongside

David Thomson's *Biographical Dictionary of Film*—which, for all its pleasures, gives an entry to Michael Bay, but not to Dalton Trumbo.

As even the following cursory roundup suggests, the evidence for a radical rewrite of American film history is thick on the ground. The Internet Movie Database continues to make those writers' filmographies easier than ever to locate.* Netflix.com, despite unconscionably failing to make its database searchable by screenwriters as well as directors, makes the films themselves easier to procure. If studios persist in releasing DVD's without screenwriters' commentaries, then somebody like the WGA simply needs to record such tracks themselves, and to stream and podcast them online. Then—once we can finally study a screenwriter's work with all the daft dedication we used to lavish on a director's—then, and only then, may the best theory win.

What follows is a lumpy, skimpy abecedary of reliably gifted screenwriters, both classic and contemporary. Readers are encouraged to regard it as a mere IOU for the comprehensive biographical dictionary of screenwriters that *schreiberism* cries out for. But, even in its ludicrously partial state,

---

* This, despite making a visitor click through to a supplemental page to learn the full authorship of movies with more than two credited writers.

the list might just help condition filmgoers to recognize and look for screenwriters' names, the way some already do for the names of directors.

To qualify for inclusion, writers had to meet three criteria. First, at least half should have credits in the past decade. No sense duplicating Richard Corliss' tactical blunder of shortchanging the current scene. In fact, many of the contemporary screenwriters below have new movies opening soon. Some of these movies will most assuredly stink, thereby jeopardizing their writers' standing in the new pantheon. If too many stink, the pantheon itself may topple. But if enough shine, or at least fail in interesting ways, they should reinforce the case for a writer-centered cosmology of film.

Second, look in vain for many writer-directors here. This condition is not imposed to impugn the frequently ambitious work coming from Robert Towne, Ron Shelton, or their like. Instead, it's intended to throw a little overdue limelight on those writers who *don't* direct—who may, in some cases, be constitutionally maladapted to direct. Many writers tend, after all, to be solitary sorts, little given to the persuasive gregariousness a director needs. A good director—and make no mistake, a good screenwriter wants a good director, just as a good novelist wants a good editor—a good director excels at telling people what to do. A good writer feels more comfortable telling fictional characters what to do, and even *they* don't always listen.

Finally, everybody listed below has at least two movies to his credit. This stipulation leaves out some gifted screenwriters just starting out, but, for the moment, these one-offs will have to wait. You can't find consistent, developing themes in a filmography with only one film in it.

THE LIST, FROM AGEE TO ZAILLIAN

JAMES AGEE (1909-1955)

One of the first things to jump out at a viewer of *The African Queen* and *Night of the Hunter*—aside from their manifest intelligence, wit, detail, and craft—is their robust anti-clericalism. Does anything in the filmographies or biographies of either picture's director (John Huston for the former or Charles Laughton the latter) chime as harmoniously as those two films do together? *African Queen* tells the story of a starchy missionary's slow unbuttoning, while *Night of the Hunter* traces a false preacher's murderous designs on two children standing between him and a fortune. In the first picture, holy scripture is an impediment to love; in the second, it's a hypocrite's prop. Even in his underrated, almost unseen 45-minute "The Bride Comes to Yellow Sky," Agee has enlarged and mocked the original figure of the village preacher. What Agee's lifelong friend Father Flye—he of the isolated Episcopal boarding school in the Appalachians that Agee was packed off to after his father's sudden death—might have said about this would be hard to divine. Admittedly, these three films began life in the imaginations of C.S. Forester, Davis Grubb, and Stephen Crane, not Agee. But as with any decent screen adapter, Agee's choices, both of materials and accentuation, betray the stamp of a true *schreiber*.

> *The Night of the Hunter* (1955)
>
> *Face to Face* (1952)
>
>   (segment "The Bride Comes to Yellow Sky")
>
> *Crin-Blanc* (1952) (commentary) w/Albert Lamorisse
>
> *The African Queen* (1951)
>
>   w/John Huston and Peter Viertel
>
> *The Quiet One* (1948)
>
>   w/Helen Levitt, Janice Loeb, and Sidney Meyers

PAUL ATTANASIO (1959-)

A former film critic for the *Washington Post*, Attanasio's credits include *Quiz Show*, *Donnie Brasco*, and a still-unfilmed biopic of Lindbergh. The recurring theme here, what Henry James called "the figure in the carpet," may be a preoccupation with ideas of assimilation—whether the narc Brasco's infiltration of a Mob family, or *Quiz Show* contestant Mark Van Doren's attempt to transcend his WASP caste and ingratiate himself into the American mainstream.

The Sum of All Fears (2002) w/Daniel Pyne
Sphere (1998) w/Kurt Wimmer and Stephen Hauser
Donnie Brasco (1997)
Disclosure (1994)
Quiz Show (1994)

BRAD BIRD (1956-)

From his earliest screen credit as a co-writer on **batteries not included*, the writer and, latterly, director Brad Bird has told stories of characters who hide their light under a bushel. In that film, it was a group of apartment-dwellers who have to protect some airborne alien gizmos from discovery. Like the boy who protects the eponymous *Iron Giant*, they are eventually repaid for their kindness with a heroic rescue. Bird's TV series "Family Dog" focused on a household pet whose intelligence also remains carefully hidden from his clueless family.

The culmination of this recurring theme of concealed talent comes in *The Incredibles*, where a family of superheroes in the witness-protection program has to hide their prodigious gifts from the mortals around them. Could all this secrecy about good fortune have something to do with what it must've been like for Bird, growing up artistically gifted in a couple of sleepy Northwestern towns? When *schreiberists* finally engage in biographical criticism, this is the sort of question they'll be asking.

The Incredibles (2004)
The Iron Giant (1999) (screen story) w/Tim McCanlies
batteries not included (1987)
    w/Matthew Robbins, Brent Maddock, and S.S. Wilson

WILLIAM BROYLES, JR. (1944-)

A former editor at *Texas Monthly* and *Newsweek* and writer-producer for the TV series *China Beach*, Broyles' feature credits include *Apollo 13*, *Cast Away*, *Planet of the Apes*, and *Jarhead*. Even the most dedicated *auteurist* would have to concede the motivic consistency of these pictures, all variations on the theme of exile and return.

Jarhead (2005)
The Polar Express (2004) w/Robert Zemeckis

Unfaithful (2002) w/Alvin Sargent
Planet of the Apes (2001)
    w/Lawrence Konner and Mark Rosenthal
Cast Away (2000)
Entrapment (1999) w/Ronald Bass
Apollo 13 (1995) w/Al Reinert
JFK: Reckless Youth (1993) (TV)

JEAN-CLAUDE CARRIERE (1931-)

Surely the only screenwriter to have worked with Luis Bunuel, Milos Forman, Volker Schlondorff, Andrzej Wajda, Philip Kaufman, Peter Brook, and Louis Malle (directors all, but not a stiff in the bunch), Carriere's many credits include *The Tin Drum, Danton, The Discreet Charm of the Bourgeoisie*, and *The Unbearable Lightness of Being*. Carriere habitually treats the plight of the individual trapped by an oppressive, claustrophobic state—perhaps not surprising in the work of a diagnosed agoraphobe.

Birth (2004) w/Milo Addica and Jonathan Glazer
Salsa (2000) w/Joyce Bunuel
La Guerre dans le Haut Pays (1999) w/Francis Reusser
Chinese Box (1997) w/Larry Gross
The Horseman on the Roof (1995)
    w/Nina Companeez and Jean-Paul Rappeneau

The Night and the Moment (1995) w/Anna-Maria Tato

Le Retour de Casanova (1992) w/Edouard Niermans

At Play in the Fields of the Lord (1991) w/Hector Babenco

Cyrano de Bergerac (1990) w/Jean-Paul Rappeneau

May Fools (1990) w/Louis Malle

Valmont (1989)

The Unbearable Lightness of Being (1988)
   w/Philip Kaufman

Swann in Love (1984)
   w/Peter Brook and Marie-Hélène Estienne

Le Retour de Martin Guerre (1982) w/Daniel Vigne

Circle of Deceit (1981)
   w/Volker Schlondorff, Margarethe von Trotta,
   and Kai Hermann

The Tin Drum (1979) w/Franz Seitz and Volker Schlondorff

Un Papillon sur l'Èpaule (1978) w/Tonino Guerra

That Obscure Object of Desire (1977) w/Luis Bunuel

The Phantom of Liberty (1974) w/Luis Bunuel

The Outside Man (1972)
   w/Jacques Deray and Ian McLellan Hunter

The Discreet Charm of the Bourgeoisie (1972)
   w/Luis Bunuel

Taking Off (1971)
   w/Milos Forman, John Guare, and John Klein

Borsalino (1970)
   w/Jean Cau, Jacques Deray, and Claude Sautet

La Voie lactée (1969) w/Luis Bunuel

Belle de jour (1967)

Hotel Paradiso (1966) w/Peter Glenville

Viva María! (1965) w/Louis Malle

Diary of a Chambermaid (1964) w/Luis Bunuel

Le Soupirant (1962) w/Pierre Etaix

PAUL DEHN (1912-1976)

The late Paul Dehn may have been the most successful pure screenwriter who ever paced. By pure I mean that he never directed, only wrote some of the smartest, most enjoyable, most lavishly visual entertainments of the postwar era; by successful, I mean that his scripts helped spawn or revive entire lucrative subgenres. Dehn's script for *Goldfinger* with Richard Maibaum has more verve and panache than predecessors *Dr. No* and *From Russia With Love* put together. "Goldfinger, do you expect me to talk?" Connery asks. "No, Mr. Bond. I expect you to die," the obscure English actor Michael Collins marvelously replies, in an invaluable contribution to the picture's success even more unsung than any screenwriter's: He's the voice actor who dubbed Gert Frobe. Great moment, just great.

A year afterward, Dehn's *The Spy Who Came In from the Cold* and *The Deadly Affair* (starring James Mason as a more than creditable George Smiley) were the first two films adapted from John LeCarre novels. Without them to demonstrate LeCarre's potential as film fodder, *The Looking Glass War*—written by the estimable Frank Pierson, of justly earned *Dog Day Afternoon* fame, but unfortunately first-time-directed by him too—might have labeled LeCarre boxoffice poison for a generation.

Likewise, before Dehn's adaptation of *The Taming of the Shrew* for Richard Burton and Elizabeth Taylor, Shakespeare's Hollywood reputation was in the dumper. Not since the Brando *Julius Caesar* and the Olivier *Richard III*, more than a decade before, had Wagstaff got anything like his cinematic due. But since *Taming of the Shrew*, hardly a year has gone by without Peter Brook, Kenneth Branagh, or somebody else trying his luck.

A year later, Dehn's sterling work on *Planet of the Apes* fired the grown-up imagination as movie science fiction has all but forgotten how to do. The movie has since sired four sequels, a television series, an animated series, and a remake, and Dehn wrote or co-wrote all four sequels. Thanks to the Writers Guild's byzantine arbitration process, what he did *not* get credit for was helping to write the original. That credit was instead ascribed to the great blacklist survivor Michael Wilson, who had done most of his best work (*The Bridge on the*

River Kwai, Lawrence of Arabia) uncredited, and to a, by 1968, rather beaten-down Rod Serling—a misattribution that even Serling's largely sympathetic biographer is openly sheepish about.

Dehn's last picture was *Murder on the Orient Express*. Before it, the last even remotely successful Agatha Christie adaptations had been a few Miss Marple adventures starring Margaret Rutherford in the early '60s. Afterward, as with Shakespeare, hardly a year has passed without somebody in film or television taking a crack at her.

From a commercial standpoint, then, Dehn comes down to us as the master prospector, finding inexhaustible gold in veins never before suspected or, more often, long thought played out. Creatively too, the Dehn stamp is hard to mistake. Dehn's first shared credit, the sophisticated, atmospheric British nuclear thriller *Seven Days to Noon*, trafficked in panoramic vistas of London under an evacuation order. Years later he was still writing unforgettable images of mass chaos, such as Goldfinger's gassing and resurrection of the guards outside Fort Knox, or the suggested nuclear holocaust from the puckish *Planet of the Apes* sequels.

Even in a more intimate, less spectacular key, Dehn retains a fascination with crowds, panic, and claustrophobia. Think of the twelve trapped suspects awaiting that snowplow aboard the Orient Express, or Dehn's spooky denouement for *A Deadly Affair*, in which a spy surrounded by a theater audience allows herself to be quietly strangled rather than risk exposing her confederate. Taken together, these sublime thrillers mark Dehn as the archpoet of the Cold War. One wishes in vain for even a bad biographical sketch of him. The only readily available information describes Paul Dehn as already a London newspaper film critic by 1936, at the age of 24. Is it asking too much, in light of his later preoccupation with desolation and escape, to wonder what sort of war he had?

Murder on the Orient Express (1974)
Battle for the Planet of the Apes (1973)
   w/John William Corrington and
   Joyce Hooper Corrington
Conquest of the Planet of the Apes (1972)
Escape from the Planet of the Apes (1971)
Fragment of Fear (1970)...aka *Freelance*
Beneath the Planet of the Apes (1970) w/Mort Abrahams
The Taming of the Shrew (1967)
   w/Suso Cecchi d'Amico and Franco Zeffirelli
The Night of the Generals (1967) w/Joseph Kessel
The Deadly Affair (1966)

The Spy Who Came In from the Cold (1965)
   w/Guy Trosper
Goldfinger (1964) w/Richard Maibaum
Orders to Kill (1958) w/George St. George
On Such a Night (1956)
Seven Days to Noon (1950) (story)
   w/James Bernard; screenplay by Roy Boulting
   and Frank Harvey

JULIUS J. EPSTEIN (1909 - 2000)

Like Charles Brackett after his break with Billy
Wilder, Julius Epstein belonged to a breed whose
current near-extinction goes a long way toward
explaining the screenwriter's diminished role in
modern Hollywood: the writer-producer. Neither
man ever took a directing credit, yet each found
properties, adapted them, and then hired directors
to implement his vision. If such a director for hire
took undue liberties with the script, no writer-
producer worth his cigar would have failed to give
him his walking papers. Nowadays, of course, the
writer-producer goes by a different name: He is a
"showrunner," and his province is not the movies,
but television.

Epstein's career forks into two halves, before
and after the death of his twin brother and writing

partner, Philip, from cancer in 1952. In the 15 years they worked as a team, the Epsteins specialized in snappy byplay and potent sentiment, with a thriving sideline in romantic triangles. Examples include a philandering Bette Davis losing her looks but finally appreciating her husband in *Mr. Skeffington*, the Cagney comedies *The Bride Came C.O.D.* and *The Strawberry Blonde*, a travesty of Salinger's "Uncle Wiggly in Connecticut" that came and went by the name of *My Foolish Heart* and—most happily—*Casablanca*.

Epstein later called that picture "slick shit," but he must at some level have cared about *Casablanca*, or he wouldn't have said, "I still have nightmares" about the narrowly averted prospect of Ronald Reagan as Rick. The movie won the Epsteins and Howard Koch an Oscar, and it's been intriguing over the years to trace fluctuations in its claim to greatness. Twenty years ago, if you'd asked someone to quote a line from *Casablanca*, almost certainly they'd've come out with "Here's looking at you, kid." Today, it's the comedy that endures. Ask again about a great line, and you're likelier to hear, "I was misinformed," or the deathless "I'm shocked—shocked!" If Julius Epstein and his brother didn't write that line, I'll eat this book.

Naturally, the loss of his brother rocked Epstein. In vain he cast around for a writing partner he could spiel with as easily as he had with Philip. He started writing romantic comedies about playboys finally settling down, like *Young at Heart* and *The Tender Trap*—possibly a reflection of his own experiences playing the field creatively, as with Billy Wilder's co-writing the "gigolo redeemed" script *Love in the Afternoon* after settling down with I.A.L. Diamond to replace his old partner Brackett.

For Epstein, alas, there would be no second soulmate. Increasingly he wrote alone, and in movies like *The Light in the Piazza* and later *Pete 'n' Tillie*, his work deepened and darkened. The capstone to his career is *Reuben, Reuben*—still unavailable on DVD, and one of those minor masterpieces whose reputation might rank much higher if the rights to it were a little less muddy and it could play almost nightly on TNT, the way Frank Darabont's still-underestimated *The Shawshank Redemption* does.

Incidentally, Epstein makes a fascinating parallel with the screenwriter Ring Lardner Jr., who, after David Lardner was killed covering World War II for the *New Yorker*, also wound up looking after his late brother's children—though only Lardner went the extra step of marrying the widow. People rightly marvel at how Lardner won Oscars twenty-eight years apart for *Woman of the Year* and *M*A*S*H*, and well they should. He came back from the blacklist—a handicap Epstein, despite his antipathy for the HUAC snitch Reagan, never had to hurdle. Yet Epstein received his Oscar for *Casablanca* and a nomination for *Pete 'n' Tillie* thirty years apart, and another nomination for *Reuben, Reuben* eleven years after that. In a profession where a decade buys you a gold watch, *that's* a career.

Reuben, Reuben (1983)
House Calls (1978) (story)
   w/Alan Mandel and Charles Shyer
Cross of Iron (1977) w/Herbert Asmodi
Jacqueline Susann's Once Is Not Enough (1975)
Pete 'n' Tillie (1972)
Return from the Ashes (1965)
Send Me No Flowers (1964)
Light in the Piazza (1962)
Fanny (1961)
Tall Story (1960)
Take a Giant Step (1959) w/Louis S. Peterson
The Reluctant Debutante (1958)
The Brothers Karamazov (1958)
Kiss Them for Me (1957)

The Tender Trap (1955)

Young at Heart (1954) w/Lenore Coffee

The Last Time I Saw Paris (1954)
   w/Philip G. Epstein and Richard Brooks

Forever Female (1953) w/Philip G. Epstein

Take Care of My Little Girl (1951) w/Philip G. Epstein

My Foolish Heart (1949) w/Philip G. Epstein

Romance on the High Seas (1948)
   w/Philip G. Epstein and I.A.L. Diamond

One More Tomorrow (1946)
   (additional dialogue) w/Philip G. Epstein,
   Charles Hoffman, and Catherine Turney

"War Comes to America" (1945)
   w/Philip G. Epstein, Anatole Litvak,
   and Anthony Veiller...aka *Why We Fight, 7*

Arsenic and Old Lace (1944) w/Philip G. Epstein

Mr. Skeffington (1944) w/Philip G. Epstein

"The Battle of China" (1944)
   w/Philip G. Epstein...aka *Why We Fight, 6*

"The Battle of Russia" (1943)
   w/Philip G. Epstein, Anatole Litvak, Anthony Veiller,
   and Robert Heller...aka *Why We Fight, 5*

"The Battle of Britain" (1943)
   w/Philip G. Epstein...aka *Why We Fight, 4*

"Divide and Conquer" (1943)
   w/Philip G. Epstein...aka *Why We Fight, 3*

"The Nazis Strike" (1943)
   w/Philip G. Epstein...aka *Why We Fight, 2*

"Prelude to War" (1943)

> w/Philip G. Epstein, Eric Knight, Anthony Veiller,
> and Robert Heller... aka *Why We Fight, 1*

Casablanca (1942) w/Philip G. Epstein and Howard Koch

Yankee Doodle Dandy (1942)

> (uncredited w/Philip G. Epstein)
> w/Robert Buckner and Edmund Joseph

The Male Animal (1942)

> w/Philip G. Epstein and Stephen Morehouse Avery

The Man Who Came to Dinner (1942) w/Philip G. Epstein

The Bride Came C.O.D. (1941) w/Philip G. Epstein

The Strawberry Blonde (1941) w/Philip G. Epstein

Honeymoon for Three (1941)

> (additional dialogue w/Philip G. Epstein) w/Earl Baldwin

No Time for Comedy (1940) w/Philip G. Epstein

Saturday's Children (1940) w/Philip G. Epstein

Four Wives (1939)

> w/Philip G. Epstein and Maurice Hanline

Daughters Courageous (1939) w/Philip G. Epstein

Secrets of an Actress (1938)

> w/Milton Krims, Rowland Leigh, Charles Kenyon,
> and Mary C. McCall Jr.

Four Daughters (1938) w/Lenore Coffee

Fools for Scandal (1938)

> (uncredited contributing writer w/Philip G. Epstein,
> Edith Fitzgerald, Robert Rossen)
> w/Herbert Fields, Joseph Fields, and Irv Brecher

Confession (1937) w/Margaret Le Vino

BENEDICT FITZGERALD (1949-)

Son of the late poet and classical translator Robert Fitzgerald, Benedict Fitzgerald has made a name for himself by sculpting scripts out of the best marble Western literature has to offer. Not for him the heedless chasing after whatever potboiler tops the bestseller charts. If Fitzgerald wants to option your book, you have definitely arrived. Unfortunately, if Fitzgerald wants to option your book, it's probably in the public domain by now, and there's no telling what domain you might be in.

What the books below have in common is a preoccupation with martyrdom, madness and the nature of evil. Ahab, Kurtz, and even Zelda all go insane in a pitiless universe, and even Jesus dares to question God at the end. In other words, despite his Penguin Classics approach to screenwriting, don't look for Fitzgerald to go adapting Jane Austen any time soon. The question is: Where was he when Warners was travestying *The Iliad* for *Troy*?

The Passion of the Christ (2004) w/Mel Gibson

Moby Dick (1998) (TV)
    w/Anton Diether and Franc Roddam

In Cold Blood (1996) (TV)

Heart of Darkness (1994) (TV)

Zelda (1993) (TV) w/Anthony Ivor

Wise Blood (1979) w/Michael Fitzgerald

TERRY GEORGE (1952-)

Writer-director George's personal imprint on *Hotel Rwanda* is hard to mistake. Like Gerry Conlon in *In the Name of the Father* and most all his other heroes, Paul Rusesabagina of *Hotel Rwanda* is essentially an apolitical man in jeopardy who discovers reserves of moral courage he never knew he had.

> *Hotel Rwanda* (2004)   w/Keir Pearson
> *Hart's War* (2002) w/Billy Ray
> *The District* (2000) TV Series (creator-writer)
> *A Bright Shining Lie* (1998) (TV)
> *The Boxer* (1997) w/Jim Sheridan
> *Some Mother's Son* (1996) w/Jim Sheridan
> *In the Name of the Father* (1993) w/Jim Sheridan

WILLIAM GOLDMAN (1931-)

A fine if atrophied novelist and screenwriting's frankest, funniest explainer to the wider world, Goldman's credits include *Butch Cassidy and the Sundance Kid* and, from his own novel, *Marathon Man*. Both pictures, and several of his other works, are partly about the counterintuitive nobility of running away: Butch and the Kid from the Superposse to Bolivia, Babe Levy from a bunch of

Nazis to the doorstep of anyone who'll let him in—
even Bob Woodward from whoever was after him in
that parking garage.

Dreamcatcher (2003) w/Lawrence Kasdan

Hearts in Atlantis (2001)

The General's Daughter (1999) w/Christopher Bertolini

Absolute Power (1997)

Fierce Creatures (1997) (uncredited)
    w/John Cleese and Iain Johnstone

The Chamber (1996)

The Ghost and the Darkness (1996)

Maverick (1994)

Chaplin (1992) w/William Boyd and Bryan Forbes

Year of the Comet (1992)

Memoirs of an Invisible Man (1992)
    w/Robert Collector and Dana Olsen

Misery (1990)

The Princess Bride (1987)

Heat (1986) (from his novel)

Mr. Horn (1979) (TV)

Magic (1978)

A Bridge Too Far (1977)

Marathon Man (1976) (from his novel)

All the President's Men (1976)

The Great Waldo Pepper (1975)

The Stepford Wives (1975)

The Hot Rock (1972)

Butch Cassidy and the Sundance Kid (1969)

No Way to Treat a Lady (1968) (from his novel)

Harper (1966)

Masquerade (1965) w/Michael Relph

SUSANNAH GRANT (1963-)

A list truly reflecting the lopsided demographics of today's successful screenwriters should probably feature two-fifths of a woman at most, but Grant has distinguished herself with credits including *Ever After* and *Erin Brockovich*. Their shared-meaning element (as *Webster's* puts it when differentiating similar but not identical words) is not just the presence of strong, underestimated women, but of men in *deus ex machina* roles—Leonardo da Vinci in the first case, Aaron Eckhardt's biker/homebody in the second.

In Her Shoes (2005)

Erin Brockovich (2000)

28 Days (2000)

Ever After (1998)

Pocahontas (1995) w/Carl Binder and Phil LaZebnik

Party of Five (1994) TV series

SIDNEY HOWARD (1891-1939)

Few people today can place the name of Sidney Howard, which just goes to show that dying young, famous, and violently doesn't always guarantee a ticket to posterity. If Howard is remembered at all, it's for adapting Margaret Mitchell's *Gone With the Wind* into a 1939 movie you may have heard of.

Any wise men present at the birth of Sidney Coe Howard in 1891 could be forgiven for leaving the frankincense at home. In the famous-playwright sweepstakes, Howard looked to have at least two strikes against him. For one, he was an Oaklander well before Jack London had put that town anywhere near America's literary map. For another, the American theater did not yet, in any sense we would now recognize, exist. Its emergence from melodrama and vaudeville into maturity still awaited the advent of another sometime East Bay denizen, Eugene O'Neill.

Yet Howard's screenplays from the '30s may just be the real undiscovered trove. His screen career ended with *Gone With the Wind*, but it by no means began there. As one of Samuel Goldwyn's pet writers, Howard authored scripts for such Ronald Colman vehicles as *Raffles*, *Bulldog Drummond*, and the unfairly unsung *Condemned*. He also helped write *Yellow Jack*, about the eradication of yellow fever, and the frankly dismal *One Heavenly Night*, but also *Arrowsmith* and *Dodsworth*, two Sinclair Lewis adaptations with which even the notoriously prickly Lewis pronounced himself pleased.

Howard's filmography hangs together far better thematically than those of any man hired to direct his scripts. His obsessions have a way of cropping up even in his most faithful adaptations—just as directors' personal signatures are alleged to, no matter how late their producers assigned them to a given project. For starters, among Howard's recurrent themes would have to be:

- the love triangle composed of two rivals widely separated in age, with a desirable third—as Tom Lehrer says in "Lobachevsky"—playing the part of hypotenuse. This theme turns up not just in *They Knew What They Wanted* and *Dodsworth*, but also in *Condemned*, about a rakish Devil's Island prisoner's affair with the warden's wife, and in Howard's gloriously hokey play *The Silver Cord*, about a smothering mother who fakes an angina attack every time her cherished son prepares to leave with his fiancée. (Redd Foxx's classic guilt-inducing groans of "Elizabeth! I'm coming!" on *Sanford & Son* owe everything to this all-but-forgotten antecedent.) Even *Gone With the Wind* can be finessed to fit this schema without excessive foot-binding, since Ashley Wilkes is plainly playing the mature fuddy-duddy to Rhett Butler's vigorously youthful rake.

- open endings that portend more than they conclude. This tendency didn't sit well with Sam Goldwyn, who tacked as tacky a resolution onto *Condemned* as he later would onto Ben Hecht's *Wuthering Heights*. *They Knew What They Wanted* and *Arrowsmith* also eschew total closure. *Arrowsmith* ends with Colman's idealistic researcher forsaking his Manhattan foundation to build his own lab in the Vermont woods. (This may have been Howard's coded kiss-off to Goldwyn in favor of Broadway—until David O. Selznick later made him an offer he couldn't refuse.)

    Then there's the most famous open ending in Hollywood history: Scarlett O'Hara's avowal that "Tomorrow is another day." No word about Rhett there, and not much about Scarlett's own future. (In today's sequel-minded Hollywood, Howard's penchant for open endings might have fared rather better.) Sure, most of this finale is straight out of the novel, but Howard could have changed it and didn't. Besides, if a director can bogart credit for writers' ideas—the old "Sure, Hecht wrote 'Notorious,' but Hitchcock chose the material" canard—then surely adapters deserve some of the same rented glory.

- finally, Howard's love of nature and the pastoral. We see this in *Arrowsmith's* ending too. You wouldn't catch a Howard hero leaving his lab in the Vermont woods for one in Manhattan, or not in the last reel, anyway.

The plays *The Silver Cord* and *They Knew What They Wanted*, the adapted mysteries *Bulldog Drummond* and *Raffles*—all turn on the opposition between the cosmopolitan and the bucolic, the removal from London society in favor of country-house intrigues. Here, too, the granddaddy of them all is *Gone With the Wind*, where early on the great Thomas Mitchell as Mr. O'Hara tells Vivien Leigh as his daughter, "Land is the only thing worth fighting for, worth dying for, because it's the only thing that lasts." It takes Scarlett nearly four hours to come around, but Howard's characteristic feel for the land wins out in the end. Scarlett loves Rhett more than Ashley, but she loves Tara more than either.

Howard's love of nature ultimately cost him his life. Far from his native Oakland, he had relocated to a hobby farm in the Berkshires, and there, just a few months shy of his unshared Oscar triumph for *Gone With the Wind*, a tractor rolled over on top of him.

At his death, Howard was only forty-eight. His daughter Jennifer later married Samuel Goldwyn Jr., making Howard the posthumous grandfather of the actor Tony Goldwyn and his producer brother, John. But of Howard's own distinctive if uneven work, too little is remembered. More movie buffs can name George Cukor for his uncredited directorial contributions to *Gone With the Wind* than they can Howard, on whose unshared credit Selznick personally insisted. Maybe land really is the only thing that lasts.

He Stayed for Breakfast (1940)
    w/Michael Fessier, Ernest Vajda,
    and P.J. Wolfson
Northwest Passage (1940)
    (uncredited w/Robert Sherwood and King Vidor)
    w/Talbot Jennings and Laurence Stallings
Raffles (1940) (1930 screenplay)
    w/John Van Druten
Gone with the Wind (1939)
The Prisoner of Zenda (1937)
    (uncredited w/Ben Hecht)
    w/Edward Rose, Wells Root, John L. Balderston,
    and Donald Ogden Stewart
Dodsworth (1936)
The Greeks Had a Word for Them (1932)
Arrowsmith (1931)
One Heavenly Night (1931)
Raffles (1930)
A Lady to Love (1930)
    (from his play *They Knew What They Wanted*)
Condemned (1929)
Bulldog Drummond (1929)

AGENORE INCROCCI (1914 - 1974)

Working as Age and Scarpelli with his usual partner, Furio Scarpelli, Incrocci has his name on two of the finest Italian movies ever to reach these shores: *Big Deal on Madonna Street* and *The Good, the Bad and the Ugly*. Each suggests a preternatural gift for transfiguring genre material, whether from a caper film into a comedy, or from a simple western into an epic. Both, meanwhile, tell a story of dishonor among thieves, with mutual distrust threatening to sabotage the conspirators' shot at a big score. There is surely more to both men (Scarpelli, for example, helped write *Il Postino*), but, pending better stateside distribution for even the cream of Italian filmmaking, this will have to do. Not the least of *auteurism*'s crimes is its tyranny over foreign film releasing, whereby any Italian film not directed by Fellini or Leone, any Japanese film not directed by Kurosawa or Ozu, any Spanish film not directed by Almadovar—no matter how well-written or engaging—stands next to no chance of getting picked up.

Boom (1999)
    w/Rodolfo Lagana, Mauro Mortaroli, Erminio Perocco, and Andrea Zaccariello
Una Botta di vita (1988)
    w/Liliane Betti, Enrico Oldoini, and Alberto Sordi

I Soliti ignoti vent'anni dopo (1987)

    w/Suso Cecchi d'Amico and Amanzio Todini...

    aka *Big Deal After 20 Years*

Scemo di guerra (1985) w/Furio Scarpelli

Le Bon roi Dagobert (1984)

Il Tassinaro (1983)

    w/Furio Scarpelli and Alberto Sordi

Scherzo del destino in agguato dietro l'angolo come un

    brigante da strada (1983) w/Lina Wertmuller

Spaghetti House (1982)

Sunday Lovers (1980)

    (segment "Armando's Notebook") w/Furio Scarpelli

Doppio delitto (1978) w/Furio Scarpelli and Steno

We All Loved Each Other So Much (1974)

    (story, screenplay, and dialogue)

    w/Furio Scarpelli and Ettore Scola

Vogliamo i colonnelli (1973)

    w/Furio Scarpelli and Mario Monicelli

Senza famiglia, nullatenenti cercano affetto (1972)

    (also story) w/Furio Scarpelli and Vittorio Gassman

In nome del popolo italiano (1971)

    (also story) w/Furio Scarpelli

Dramma della gelosia—tutti i particolari in cronaca (1970)

    w/Furio Scarpelli and Ettore Scola

Situation Normal, All Fouled Up (1970)

    (also story) w/Furio Scarpelli and Nanni Loy

Straziami, ma di baci saziami (1968) (also story)

    w/Furio Scarpelli and Dino Risi

(AGENORE INCROCCI CONTINUED)

Riusciranno i nostri eroi a ritrovare l'amico
   misteriosamente scomparso in Africa? (1968)
   (also story) w/Furio Scarpelli and Ettore Scola
Capriccio all'italiana (1968)
   (segments "La Bambinaia," "Viaggio di lavoro,"
   "Perché?") w/Furio Scarpelli
Il Tigre (1967)
   w/Furio Scarpelli, John O. Douglas, and Dino Risi
Ti ho sposato per allegria (1967)
   w/Sandro Continenza, Natalia Ginzburg,
   and Luciano Salce
The Good, the Bad and the Ugly (1966)
   w/ Furio Scarpelli, Luciano Vincenzoni, and Sergio Leone
Casanova '70 (1965)
   w/Furio Scarpelli, Suso Cecchi d'Amico,
   Giorgio Salvioni, and Mario Monicelli
Sedotta e abbandonata (1964)
   (dialogue) w/Furio Scarpelli, Pietro Germi,
   and Luciano Vincenzoni
I Compagni (1963) w/Furio Scarpelli and Mario Monicelli
The Best of Enemies (1962)
   w/Furio Scarpelli, Suso Cecchi d'Amico, Jack Pulman,
   and Luciano Vincenzoni
A cavallo della tigre (1961)
   (also story) w/Furio Scarpelli, Luigi Comencini,
   and Mario Monicelli

Divorce—Italian Style (1961)

    (uncredited) w/Ennio De Concini, Pietro Germi,

    and Alfredo Giannetti

Risate di gioia (1960)

    w/Furio Scarpelli, Mario Monicelli,

    and Suso Cecchi d'Amico

Audace colpo dei soliti ignoti (1959)

    (also story) w/Furio Scarpelli and Nanni Loy

La Grande guerra (1959)

    w/Furio Scarpelli, Mario Monicelli,

    and Luciano Vincenzoni

Policarpo, ufficiale di scrittura (1959)

    w/Furio Scarpelli, Arnaldo Gandolini,

    and Antonio Navarro Linares

Big Deal on Madonna Street (1958)

    (story) w/Furio Scarpelli, Suso Cecchi d'Amico,

    and Mario Monicelli

Primo amore (1958) w/Ettore Scola

Souvenir d'Italie (1957)

    w/Furio Scarpelli, Dario Fo, and Antonio Pietrangeli

Padri e figli (1957)

    w/Furio Scarpelli, Mario Monicelli, Leonardo Benvenuti,

    and Luigi Emmanuele

La Banda degli onesti (1956) w/Furio Scarpelli

Il Bigamo (1956)

    w/Furio Scarpelli, Sergio Amidei, Francesco Rosi,

    and Vincenzo Talarico

Racconti romani (1955)

>   w/Furio Scarpelli, Sergio Amidei, Francesco Rosi,
>   and Alberto Moravia

Totò e Carolina (1955)

>   w/Furio Scarpelli, Rodolfo Sonego, Mario Monicelli,
>   and Ennio Flaiano

Sinfonia d'amore (1954)

>   w/Liana Ferri and Glauco Pellegrini

Tempi nostri (1954)

>   (story "La macchina fotografica")
>   w/Furio Scarpelli and Sandro Continenza

Capitan Fantasma (1953)

>   w/Furio Scarpelli, Gino De Santis, and Primo Zeglio

A fil di spada (1952)

>   (also story) w/Furio Scarpelli and Leonardo Benvenuti

I Tre corsari (1952)

>   w/Furio Scarpelli, Ennio De Concini, and Emilio Salgari

Totò e le donne (1952)

>   w/Furio Scarpelli, Mario Monicelli, and Steno

NEAL JIMENEZ (1960-)

A graduate of the UCLA screenwriting department (whose graduates, correlated against their crosstown rivals from USC, would offer still another way to reshuffle recent film history for further study), Jimenez's credits include *River's Edge* and

The Waterdance. In both examples, characters confront the inexplicable—the motiveless murder of a teenager by her boyfriend, a writer's semi-autobiographical sudden paralysis—and have dispiriting, unromantic sex before attaining some measure of compromised grace.

Hideaway (1995) w/Andrew Kevin Walker
Sleep with Me (1994)
    w/Duane Dell'Amico, Roger Hedden, Joe Keenan,
    Rory Kelly, and Michael Steinberg
The Waterdance (1992)
For the Boys (1991)
    (story) w/Lindy Laub and Marshall Brickman
The Dark Wind (1991) w/Eric Bergren
Where the River Runs Black (1986) w/Peter Silverman
River's Edge (1986)

CHARLIE KAUFMAN (1958-)

The crotchety but invaluable Internet Movie Database notes that Charlie Kaufman's protagonists usually start out in the story as "downtrodden or self-doubtful, frustrated with life, love or their professions." While this is fine as far as it goes, and marks the rare attempt outside the WGA's monthly magazine, *Written By*, to see a screenwriter's career whole, it doesn't really get into Kaufman's continuing preoccupation with ideas of freedom and control. From John Cusack's life as a puppeteer in *Being John Malkovich*, to Chuck Barris' exploitation by his CIA controller, to the screenwriter brothers' fallible efforts to dictate their characters' lives in *Adaptation* to, finally, the laboratory boffins' manipulation of both Jim Carrey in *Eternal Sunshine of the Spotless Mind* and a grown-up wild child in *Human Nature*, all of Kaufman's films have told the story of a puppet's wish to pull his own strings.

Eternal Sunshine of the Spotless Mind (2004)
   w/Michel Gondry and Pierre Bismuth
Confessions of a Dangerous Mind (2002)
Adaptation (2002)
Human Nature (2001)
Being John Malkovich (1999)
The Dana Carvey Show (1996) TV Series
Get a Life (1990) TV Series

JOHN LOGAN (1963-)

Originally a Chicago playwright, Logan has plainly carved out a specialty writing outsized, flamboyant characters, often from mythic if not downright mythological models. The three obvious examples here are Howard Hughes, Orson Welles, and William Randolph Hearst, but as good a case could easily be made for Sinbad and Picard, for the hypocritical pacifist warriors of *The Last Samurai* and *Gladiator*, and for *Any Given Sunday*'s gridiron Lear. Typically, some of Logan's heroes peak early and, like Hughes and Welles, spend the rest of their lives trying to fulfill their own boy-wonder promise.

The Aviator (2004)
The Last Samurai (2003)
    w/Edward Zwick and Marshall Herskovitz
Sinbad: Legend of the Seven Seas (2003)
Star Trek: Nemesis (2002) w/Rick Berman and Brent Spiner
The Time Machine (2002) w/David Duncan
Gladiator (2000) w/David Franzoni and William Nicholson
Any Given Sunday (1999) w/Daniel Pyne and Oliver Stone
RKO 281 (1999) (TV)
Bats (1999)
Tornado! (1996) (TV)

RICHARD MATHESON (1926-)

The alpha and *zelig* of American genre screenwriting is this unassuming gentleman, still writing away in the west San Fernando Valley. With Rod Serling and Charles Beaumont, Matheson wrote almost all the great *Twilight Zone* TV shows, including one that, in a fairer world, would suffice to secure his immortality: *Nick of Time*. That's the one where William Shatner and Phyllis Thaxter stop in a small-town diner for a bite of lunch and become paralyzed by the Delphic pronouncements of a diabolical coin-operated tabletop fortune-teller. Only at the end do they resolve that the future is theirs to determine, not some infernal gumball machine's—even as another couple takes their table and falls prey to the exact same spell they've just escaped. Here and in *The Incredible Shrinking Man*, as with Paddy Chayefsky in *Altered States* and *The Americanization of Emily*, Matheson embodies pulp existentialism at its finest.

> *Stir of Echoes* (1999) (from his novel)
> *What Dreams May Come* (1998) (from his novel)
> *Trilogy of Terror II* (1996) (TV)
>   (also story *Prey*)
>   w/Dan Curtis, Henry Kuttner, and William F. Nolan
> *The Outer Limits* (1995) TV Series (episode "First Anniversary")
> *The Dreamer of Oz: The L. Frank Baum Story* (1990)
>   (story and teleplay) w/David Kirschner
> *Loose Cannons* (1990)
>   w/Richard Christian Matheson and Bob Clark

The Twilight Zone (1985)   (episode "Button, Button")

Jaws 3-D (1983)
  w/Carl Gottlieb, Michael Kane, and Guerdon Trueblood

Twilight Zone: The Movie (1983)
  (screenplay "Nightmare at 20,000 Feet,"
  from his short story)

The Incredible Shrinking Woman (1981)
  (from his novel *The Incredible Shrinking Man*)

The Martian Chronicles (1980) (miniseries)

Somewhere in Time (1980)
  (from his novel *Bid Time Return*)

The Strange Possession of Mrs. Oliver (1977) (TV)

Dead of Night (1977)

Trilogy of Terror (1975) (TV)
  (also story *Prey*) w/William F. Nolan

The Stranger Within (1974) (TV) (also story)

Icy Breasts (1974)
  (from his novel *Someone is Bleeding*) w/Georges
  Lautner

The Morning After (1974) (TV)

Scream of the Wolf (1974) (TV) w/David Case

Dying Room Only (1973) (TV)

The Legend of Hell House (1973) (from his novel *Hell
  House*)

The Night Strangler (1973) (TV)

Dracula (1973) (TV)

Ghost Story (1972) TV Series (episode "The New House")

The Night Stalker (1972) (TV)

Ghost Story (1972) (TV) w/Elizabeth M. Walter

Duel (1971) (TV) (also story)

The Omega Man (1971) (from his novel *I Am Legend*)

De la part des copains (1970)

    (from his novel *Ride the Nightmare*)...aka Cold Sweat

Night Gallery (1970) TV Series

    (short story and episode "Big Surprise")

    (short story and episode "The Funeral")

De Sade (1969)

It's Alive! (1969) (TV)

    (story "Being") (uncredited) w/Larry Buchanan

The Devil Rides Out (1968)

The Young Warriors (1967) (from his novel *The Beardless*
    Warriors)

Soy leyenda (1967) (from his novel *I Am Legend*)

Star Trek (1966) TV Series (episode "The Enemy Within")

Die! Die! My Darling! (1965)

The Last Man on Earth (1964)

    (from his novel *I Am Legend*) (as Logan Swanson)

    w/William Leicester, Furio M. Monetti,

    and Ubaldo Ragona

The Comedy of Terrors (1964)

Bob Hope Presents the Chrysler Theatre (1963)

    (episode "Time of Flight")

The Raven (1963)

Combat! (1962)

    (episode "Forgotten Front") (as Logan Swanson)

The Alfred Hitchcock Hour (1962) (one episode)

Edgar Allan Poe's Tales of Terror (1962)

Night of the Eagle (1962)
    w/Charles Beaumont and George Baxt

Pit and the Pendulum (1961)

Master of the World (1961)

House of Usher (1960)

The Twilight Zone (1959) TV Series

The Beat Generation (1959) w/Lewis Meltzer

Have Gun—Will Travel (1957) TV Series

The Incredible Shrinking Man (1957)
    (from his novel *The Shrinking Man*)

DUDLEY NICHOLS (1895-1960)

That intoxicating cinematic elegist David Thomson would have us believe Dudley Nichols once admitted, "A script is only a blueprint—the director is the one who makes the picture." And whom does Thomson source for this choice piece of screenwriting Uncle Tomism? Fritz Lang, who directed Nichols' scripts for *Man Hunt* and *Scarlet Street*—and why would *he* lie? Whatever the veracity of the notoriously mythomaniacal Lang, Nichols remains a great open secret and unworked seam of American film history. The only screenwriter ever to write for John Ford, Howard Hawks, Jean Renoir, Rene Clair, Leo McCarey, Elia Kazan,

Cecil B. DeMille, Anthony Mann, *and* George Cukor, Nichols worked in just about every genre. After the semi-obligatory start in journalism, Nichols came to Hollywood and excelled at dramas (*The Informer*), comedies (*Bringing Up Baby*), westerns (*Stagecoach*) , and mysteries. The last category includes an unsung miracle of the adapter's art, *And Then There Were None*, which takes a classic narrated by a dead man and somehow turns it into a romantic thriller—without either shortchanging the original or cheating the audience. Not until (Robert's brother) Roger Towne and Phil Dusenberry's script for *The Natural* has an uplifting ending been so happily engineered from such unpromising materials.

At his best, Nichols worked endless variations on a single recurring theme: the crucible of close quarters. Look at *The Lost Patrol*, in which a dozen World War I British doughboys in what is now Iraq run a desert gauntlet of snipers to rejoin their brigade. Look at *Stagecoach*, for which *The Lost Patrol* represents a sort of guys-only dry run. Or *The Long Voyage Home*, in which sailors aboard a freighter fight the elements and each other to reach safe harbor. The most perfect distillation of this theme may be *And Then There Were None*, for which Nichols had to tinker not just with Agatha

Christie's original title of *Ten Little Niggers*, but also with her unforgiving determinism. Where Christie's narrator confines his victims to an island and kills them off one by one until the last two kill each other, Nichols characteristically allows that the pressure of events can also lead to grace, courage, even love.

Despite all this, the usually unhoodwinkable Thomson leads his *Biographical Dictionary of Film* entry on Nichols not with any of his screenplays, but with the three undistinguished films he directed. This is tantamount to judging Satchel Paige on the six years he pitched as a middle-aged man in the majors, rather than the twenty-four dazzling ones he logged in the Negro Leagues. Even for as good a critic as Thomson, screenwriting remains the minors. Directing is the show. The main difference between the continuing crusade of screenwriters for respect and that of black athletes for equality is that the screenwriter has usually wanted to direct, while the black ballplayer has never especially wanted to be white.

Heller in Pink Tights (1960) w/Walter Bernstein,
The Hangman (1959) w/Luke Short and W.R. Burnett
The Tin Star (1957) w/Joel Kane and Barney Slater
Run for the Sun (1956) w/Roy Boulting

(DUDLEY NICHOLS CONTINUED)

Prince Valiant (1954)

The Big Sky (1952)

Return of the Texan (1952)

Rawhide (1951)

Pinky (1949) w/Philip Dunne

Mourning Becomes Electra (1947)

The Fugitive (1947)

Sister Kenny (1946)
    w/Mary McCarthy, Alexander Knox,
    and Milton Gunzburg

Scarlet Street (1945)

The Bells of St. Mary's (1945)

And Then There Were None (1945)

The Sign of the Cross (1944)
    (uncredited prologue)
    w/Waldemar Young and Sidney Buchman

It Happened Tomorrow (1944)
    w/Hugh Wedlock Jr., Helene Fraenkel, and Rene Clair

Government Girl (1943)
    w/Budd Schulberg and Adela Rogers St. John

For Whom the Bell Tolls (1943)

This Land Is Mine (1943)

Air Force (1943)
    w/Leah Baird and William Faulkner (uncredited)

The Battle of Midway (1942)
    w/James K. McGuinness and John Ford

Swamp Water (1941)

Man Hunt (1941)

The Long Voyage Home (1940)

The Marshal of Mesa City (1939)
    (uncredited) w/Jack Lait Jr.

Stagecoach (1939) w/Ben Hecht (uncredited)

Gunga Din (1939)
    (uncredited w/Lester Cohen, John Colton, William
    Faulkner, Vincent Lawrence, and Anthony Veiller)
    w/Ben Hecht, Charles MacArthur, Joel Sayre,
    and Fred Guiol

Trailer Romance (1938)
    (uncredited) w/John Twist and Helen Meinardi

Carefree (1938)
    (story w/Marian Ainslee, Guy Endore, and Hagar Wilde
    w/Ernest Pagano and Allan Scott)

Bringing Up Baby (1938) w/Hagar Wilde

The Hurricane (1937)
    w/Oliver H.P. Garrett and Ben Hecht (uncredited)

The Toast of New York (1937) w/John Twist and Joel Sayre

The Plough and the Stars (1936)

Mary of Scotland (1936) w/Mortimer Offner (uncredited)

The Three Musketeers (1935) w/Rowland V. Lee

Steamboat Round the Bend (1935) w/Lamar Trotti

The Crusades (1935)
    w/Harold Lamb and Waldemar Young

She (1935) (additional dialogue) w/Ruth Rose,

The Arizonian (1935)   (story)

The Informer (1935)

Life Begins at Forty (1935)

    (uncredited w/William M. Conselman)

    w/Lamar Trotti and Robert Quillen

Mystery Woman (1935) (story)

    w/Philip MacDonald and Edward E. Paramore Jr.

Marie Galante (1934) (uncredited) w/Reginald Berkeley

Judge Priest (1934) w/Lamar Trotti and Irvin S. Cobb

Call It Luck (1934)

Wild Gold (1934)

    (story) w/Lester Cole, Henry Johnson, and Lamar Trotti

Hold That Girl (1934) w/Lamar Trotti

The Lost Patrol (1934)

    w/Philip MacDonald and Garrett Fort

You Can't Buy Everything (1934)

    w/Lamar Trotti, Eve Greene, and Zelda Sears

Price of a Kiss (1933) w/Francisco More de la Torre

Pilgrimage (1933) (dialogue)

    w/Barry Conners and Philip Klein

The Man Who Dared (1933) w/Lamar Trotti

Hot Pepper (1933) (story)

    w/Barry Conners and Philip Klein

Robbers' Roost (1932)

This Sporting Age (1932) w/James K. McGuinness

Skyline (1931)

    w/William Anthony McGuide and Kenyon Nicholson

Hush Money (1931)

    w/Philip Klein, Sidney Lanfield, and Courtney Terrett

The Black Camel (1931)
    w/Barry Conners, Philip Klein, and Hugh Stange
Three Rogues (1931) w/William M. Conselman
Seas Beneath (1931) w/James Parker Jr.
A Devil with Women (1930) w/Henry Johnson
One Mad Kiss (1930) w/Adolf Paul
On the Level (1930)
    w/Andrew Bennison and William K. Wells
Born Reckless (1930)
Men Without Women (1930)

JOHN OSBORNE (1929-1994)

The subtitle of this book is *A Radical Rewrite of American Film History* for a fairly simple reason. To call it a rewrite of *Film History*, full stop, suggests the fuller understanding of international cinema that, despite the inclusions of Jean-Claude Carriere and Agenore Incrocci, I only wish I could claim. Ignorance is bad enough without pretending to omniscience. But the very use of the locution "full stop" should probably clue the reader in that my ignorance is every bit as spotty and uneven as what passes for my erudition. I remain, in common with many other halfway intelligent Americans whose parents watched *Masterpiece Theater*—or at least dozed off to it—an unrepentant anglophile.

For a lot of anglophiles, though, Blighty's cultural supremacy ended around the same time as her naval supremacy. Even Alistair Cooke, who sometimes seemed as if he had taken American citizenship the better to cultivate his anglophilia, betrayed a distinct preference for period pieces. So, in later years, did John Osborne, who was the U.K.'s first significant postwar playwright, and will have to stand in for an almost forgotten generation of terrific British screenwriters.

Contemplating the hidden riches of the pre-globalization, and especially pre-1968, British film industry is almost as much of a through-the-looking glass experience as first considering the *schreiber* theory. The initial response may be something akin to vertigo, at the sheer profusion of great-sounding English-language feature films that one has barely even heard of. Who knew, for instance, that the same Missourian who wrote *The Russians Are Coming*, *The Russians Are Coming*, and *It's a Mad, Mad, Mad, Mad World*, William Rose, also wrote the British farces *The Ladykillers*, *Genevieve*, and a charming-sounding *Cinema Paradiso* precursor called *The Smallest Show on Earth*? Or that Charlie Kaufman has a screenwriting namesake, just like his alter ego in *Adaptation*, except that *this* Charles Kaufman wrote a dozen

British films in the 1950s before earning Oscar and WGA nominations for John Huston's *Freud*? Or that a screenwriter named Nigel Kneale, the father of Booker-winning novelist Matthew Kneale, co-adapted the John Osborne plays *Look Back in Anger* and *The Entertainer* before turning to Quatermass thrillers like *Five Million Years to Earth* to keep young Matthew in digestive biscuits?

OK, so it's easy to get carried away about a lot of movies that even Netflix doesn't know from *Adam at 6 A.M.* Practically the only way for an admittedly obsessive American to know any of this is by consulting the rolls of the British Academy of Film and Television Arts Awards, for which all the above writers frequently competed. So productive was the old British film industry that between 1954 and 1968, BAFTA annually filled out a category with nominees for "Best *British* Screenplay." In 1963, for example, the year Osborne won for *Tom Jones*, he did so only by besting Keith Waterhouse and Willis Hall (*Billy Liar*) and fellow playwrights Harold Pinter (*The Servant*) and David Storey (*This Sporting Life*). No one should seriously undertake a full *schreiberist* rewrite of anglophone film history without a thorough look at all these nominees and their neglected countrymen, including Harold Pinter, the first *schreiber* to win a Nobel Prize. In their stead, Osborne will have to do.

> *England, My England* (1995) w/Charles Wood
> *A Better Class of Person* (1985) (TV)
> *God Rot Tunbridge Wells* (1985) (TV)
> *Very Like a Whale* (1981)
> *You're Not Watching Me, Mummy* (1980) (TV)
> *The Picture of Dorian Gray* (1976) (TV)
> *Almost a Vision* (1976) (TV)
> *The Gift of Friendship* (1974) (TV)
> *Ms or Jill and Jack* (1974) (TV)
> *The Right Prospectus* (1970) (TV)
> *Inadmissible Evidence* (1968) (from his play)
> *Tom Jones* (1963)
> *The Entertainer* (1960) (from his play) w/Nigel Kneale
> *Look Back in Anger* (1958) (from his play) w/Nigel Kneale

DAVID WEBB PEOPLES (1940-)

A former film and sound editor, Peoples' credits include *Blade Runner*, *12 Monkeys*, and *Unforgiven*. All three follow laconic, violent, disillusioned men who take on a dirty job, meet up with an innocent—a doe-eyed secretary, say, or an aspiring gunfighter—and survive a horrific trial to win a measure of redemption.

Soldier (1998)

Twelve Monkeys (1995) w/Janet Peoples

Hero (1992) w/Alvin Sargent and Laura Ziskin

Unforgiven (1992)

The Blood of Heroes (1990)

Fatal Sky (1990)
  (as Anthony Able) w/Brian Williams and David White

Leviathan (1989) (story) w/Jeb Stuart

Ladyhawke (1985)
  w/Edward Khmara, Michael Thomas,
  and Tom Mankiewicz

Star Wars: Episode VI—Return of the Jedi (1983)
  (uncredited)

Blade Runner (1982) w/Hampton Fancher

The Day After Trinity (1980) w/Jon Else, Janet Peoples

PAUL QUARRINGTON (1953-)

If Quarrington would just put aside his acclaimed sidelines as a novelist, folksinger and duff painter to concentrate on screenwriting, he might be even more obscure than he is now. It doesn't help that he's Canadian, a nationality only recently coming into its own as a producer of anything besides documentaries, animated shorts, and Canadian-American comedians. But Quarrington's script for *Whale Music*, based on his novel, is a marvel of character observation and unforced uplift. The story of a Brian Wilson-like reclusive musician trying to write again, *Whale Music* shares with Quarrington's script for Jessica Tandy's last film, *Camilla*, a fascination with discarded lives, and a humane hope for the written-off, the given-up-on. How Canadian, and how refreshing.

> *Chilly Beach* (2003) TV Series
>
> *1-800-Missing* (2003) TV Series
>
> *Men with Brooms* (2002)
>
> *Tom Stone* (2002) TV Series
>
> *Power Play* (1998) TV Series
>
> *Camilla* (1994) w/Ali Jennings
>
> *Whale Music* (1994) w/Richard J. Lewis
>
> *Perfectly Normal* (1990) w/Eugene Lipinski

FREDERIC RAPHAEL (1931-)

Also an accomplished novelist and classicist, the Chicago-born Raphael's credits include *Darling*, *Two for the Road* and the nonpareil British miniseries *The Glittering Prizes*. Our foremost romantic coroner, Raphael frequently concerns himself with the decay of love—usually over an extended or fractured time scheme, preferably among the rich, and frequently marked by a stinging facility of language in both dialogue and self-lacerating monologue.

Coast to Coast (2004) (TV) (from his novel)

Hiding Room (2002)

This Man, This Woman (2002)

Eyes Wide Shut (1999) w/Stanley Kubrick

Picture Windows (1995)
   (miniseries) (episode "Armed Response")

La Putain du roi (1990) w/Axel Corti and Daniel Vigne

Women and Men: Stories of Seduction (1990) (TV)

After the War (1989) (miniseries)

Oxbridge Blues (1984)
   (miniseries) TV Series
   (from his books *Oxbridge Blues* and *Sleeps Six*)

Richard's Things (1980) (from his novel)

The Best of Friends (1980) TV Series

School Play (1979) (TV)

Of Mycenae and Men (1979) (TV)

Oresteia (1979) (miniseries w/Kenneth McLeish

The Glittering Prizes (1976) (miniseries)

Rogue Male (1976) (TV)

Daisy Miller (1974)

A Severed Head (1970)

Far from the Madding Crowd (1967)

Two for the Road (1967)

Darling (1965)

Nothing But the Best (1964)

Don't Bother to Knock (1961)
   w/Denis Cannan and Frederic Gotfurt

Bachelor of Hearts (1958) w/Leslie Bricusse

ERIC ROTH (1945-)

Every great critical methodology has at least one inexplicable exception. For *auteurism*, it's how a competent journeyman like Michael Curtiz could have made *Casablanca*. (When we consider that Howard Koch and the Epstein brothers wrote it, Curtiz's achievement becomes a skootch more explicable.) For the *schreiber* theory, it's how a thoughtful screenwriter like Eric Roth, with intelligent scripts including *Forrest Gump* and *The Insider* to his credit, could ever have written *The Concorde: Airport '79*. The former pair both explore the problematic idea of ill-founded trust—a corporation's trust in an employee, a whistle-blower's trust in a journalist, a simpleton's trust in the world's goodwill.

Ali (2001)

The Insider (1999)

The Horse Whisperer (1998)

The Postman (1997) w/Brian Helgeland

Forrest Gump (1994)

Jane's House (1994) (TV)

Mr. Jones (1993) w/Michael Cristofer

Memories of Me (1988) w/Billy Crystal

Suspect (1987)

Wolfen (1981) (uncredited)

The Onion Field (1979) (uncredited)

The Concorde: Airport '79 (1979)

The Drowning Pool (1975) (uncredited)

The Nickel Ride (1974)

Strangers in 7A (1972) (TV)

To Catch a Pebble (1970)

AARON SORKIN (1961-)

For Sorkin, as for Paul Attanasio, William Broyles Jr., Larry Gelbart (*M*A*S*H*), Joss Whedon (*Buffy the Vampire Slayer*), and so many others, the siren song of television's more frequent paychecks and (relatively) smaller hassles with directors has proven hard to resist. Sorkin's credits include *The American President* and the adaptation of his play *A Few Good Men*, plus the television series *Sports Night* and *The West Wing*. Linking them all is a weakness for snappy byplay straight out of Jules Furthman, and a tendency to dramatize the writing process onscreen. His principal achievements to date are two movies about writing legal briefs and legislation, and two network series about writing sports news and political speeches. Now *that's* consistency.

The West Wing (1999) TV Series (creator)

Sports Night (1998) TV Series (creator)

The American President (1995)

Malice (1993) w/Scott Frank

A Few Good Men (1992) (from his play)

PETER STONE (1930-)

An industry kid whose parents helped write and produce the old Tom Mix westerns, Peter Stone was born in Los Angeles. He first came to my attention when I noticed that three of my favorite movies were all written by the same man: 1) *Charade*, starring Cary Grant, Audrey Hepburn, Walter Matthau, James Coburn, nebbishy Ned Glass, a one-armed George Kennedy, and, not least, Paris at its most celestial; 2) *Skin Game*, starring James Garner and Lou Gossett Jr. as two 19th-century Southern con men, one of whom keeps selling the other into slavery, then busting him back out again; and 3) *The Taking of Pelham One Two Three*, also starring Matthau—who had previously stolen the movie of Stone's script *Mirage* clean out from under its granite-hewn star, Gregory Peck.

Charade and *Skin Game* are original scripts, *Pelham One Two Three* an adaptation of John Godey's novel, but they're all a lot more unmistakably the work of the same writer than, say, *Skin Game* and *I Was a Communist for the FBI* are of the same director (Gordon Douglas, for anybody keeping score).

Charade, Skin Game and *Pelham One Two Three* are all essays in deception—tightly plotted, uproariously funny, and deeply irreverent. All their characters have one or more pseudonyms, reflecting Stone's own career-long preoccupation with masks and identity. He had at least two pseudonyms of his own, Peter Joshua and the not exactly impenetrable Pierre Marton.

Stone also had a thing about mortality, and wrote a couple of the great death scenes in modern movie history. I'm thinking of Robert Shaw as the British mercenary turned subway hijacker, cornered and turning to Matthau inside a deserted tunnel at the end of *Pelham One Two Three* to ask, "Do you still execute in this state?" Matthau, with his best quizzical bassett hound look, harrumphs, "Execute? Nah, not anymore, no." Shaw answers simply, "Pity," and kisses the side of one loafer to the third rail.

Or consider George Kennedy's demise in *Charade*. Kennedy—playing a thug with a hook for his right hand, a scowl for hello, and the glorious name of Herman Skoby—is found in his bathtub, drowned in his pajamas. His partners in crime promptly set about making it look like an accident. Ned Glass, as the no less gloriously monikered Leopold W. Gideon, suggests, "We could put him back in his bed and pretend it was a heart attack. He really doesn't look too bad." Then James Coburn as the sadistic cowboy Tex Penthollow comes out with the perfect brief eulogy, uncontemplative yet somehow unforgettable: "Seems like Herman and good luck always was strangers. Well, maybe he'll meet up with his other hand someplace."

Peter Stone and good luck were by no means strangers. He was married to the same woman for 46 years. He won an Emmy for writing a script of "The Defenders," an Oscar with Frank Tarloff for *Father Goose*, and enough Tonys for a Mafia funeral: *Titanic*, *Woman of the Year*, and his imperishable *1776*.

In 1995 or so, I did a phoner with Stone for the long-suffering *L.A. Daily News*, to coincide with a County Museum screening of *Charade* and the release of a pretty minor Sean Connery thriller called *Just Cause*. Stone had just shared script credit on the Connery picture—this at an age when most screenwriters have long since been put out to pasture. As I remember, Stone was funny, cranky, and a little surprised that anyone in his hometown had bothered to notice his work. He called me for a copy afterward, and, to my everlasting regret—out of some dumb journalist's combination of shyness, haste, and shame that it should have been better—

I never sent it to him. I always hoped I'd meet up with him someday, but it never happened, and he died in 2003.

Somebody should really come out with a DVD box set of Stone's career, the way they stubbornly keep doing with directors' filmographies. That way, other movie lovers could finally recognize and appreciate this unmistakable comic voice. Then, to paraphrase James Coburn, maybe Stone'll finally meet up with his rightful audience someplace.

Just Cause (1995) w/Jeb Stuart

Grand Larceny (1987)

Woman of the Year (1984) (TV)

Why Would I Lie? (1980)

Who Is Killing the Great Chefs of Europe? (1978)

Silver Bears (1978)

One of My Wives Is Missing (1976) (TV) (as Pierre Marton)

The Taking of Pelham One Two Three (1974)

Free to Be. . . You & Me (1974) (TV) (stories)

Adam's Rib (1973) TV Series

1776 (1972) (from his play)

Skin Game (1971)
   (as Pierre Marton) w/Richard Alan Simmons

Sweet Charity (1969)

Jigsaw (1968)

The Secret War of Harry Frigg (1968) w/Frank Tarloff

Androcles and the Lion (1967) (TV)

Ghostbreakers (1967) (TV)

Arabesque (1966) (as Pierre Marton)

Mirage (1965)

Father Goose (1964) w/Frank Tarloff

Charade (1963)   (story w/Marc Behm)

Espionage (1963) TV Series
   (episode "A Covenant with Death")

The Defenders (1961) TV Series

Studio One (1948) TV Series

TED TALLY (1952-)

Author of the terrific play *Terra Nova* (about the practical Norseman Roald Amundsen's defeat of doomed, chivalrous Englishman Robert Falcon Scott in the race for the South Pole), Tally's screen credits include *The Silence of the Lambs* and *All the Pretty Horses*. As mentioned earlier, all three describe a kind of Gotterdammerung, a twilight not of gods, but of godlike men and the passing of their courtly ways. These include the cowboy way, the Victorian way and the Lecter way, by which a serial killer's victims are not brutally slaughtered, but sautéed.

Red Dragon (2002)

All the Pretty Horses (2000)

Before and After (1996)

The Juror (1996)

The Silence of the Lambs (1991)

White Palace (1990) w/Alvin Sargent

The Father Clements Story (1987) (TV) w/Arthur Heinemann

ELWOOD ULLMAN

Ullman is far from the best screenwriter in this book, but with half a dozen Three Stooges movies, a couple of Ma and Pa Kettles and both *The Ghost in the Invisible Bikini* and *Dr. Goldfoot and the Bikini Machine* among his 130 or so screen credits, he may just be the most prolific. Like John Osborne for a generation of unsung British screenwriters, let Ullman stand in for a whole generation of contract comedy writers who were funny on demand, eight hours a day, five days a week and on call weekends.

Pending a radical reappraisal of his script for, say, the Bowery Boys picture *Dig That Uranium* (1956), at least recognize Elwood Ullman for what he was: a television writer—with all the yuks on short notice that the term implies—before there was television. Ullman also deserves to be remembered as something other than the second-best screen-writer to grow up heir to a whiskey distillery. (The best is plainly Allan Scott, who adapted Daphne du Maurier's *Don't Look Now*, Henry Fielding's *Joseph Andrews* and a sublime all-ages script for

Roald Dahl's *The Witches*—and who supervised, until recently, his family's Macallan holdings.)

The Three Stooges Follies (1974) (segment)

The Ghost in the Invisible Bikini (1966)

Dr. Goldfoot and the Bikini Machine (1965)

Tickle Me (1965)

The Outlaws Is Coming (1965)

The Three Stooges Scrapbook (1963)

The Three Stooges Go Around the World in a Daze (1963)

The Three Stooges in Orbit (1962)

The Three Stooges Meet Hercules (1962)

Snow White and the Three Stooges (1961)

Battle Flame (1959)

The Bloody Brood (1959)

In the Money (1958)

Looking for Danger (1957)

Guns A-Poppin (1957)

Spook Chasers (1957)

Footsteps in the Night (1957)

Chain of Evidence (1957)

Hot Shots (1956)

Scheming Schemers (1956)

Fighting Trouble (1956)

Dig That Uranium (1956)

Sudden Danger (1955)

Hot Ice (1955)

Jail Busters (1955)

Ma and Pa Kettle at Waikiki (1955)

High Society (1955)

Bowery to Bagdad (1955)

Scotched in Scotland (1954)

Jungle Gents (1954)

The Bowery Boys Meet the Monsters (1954)

Paris Playboys (1954)

Private Eyes (1953)

Hot News (1953)

Clipped Wings (1953)

Loose in London (1953)

The Stooge (1953)

Lost in Alaska (1952)

Ghost Buster (1952)

Listen, Judge (1952)

Harem Girl (1952)

Gold Raiders (1951)

Three Arabian Nuts (1951)

A Snitch in Time (1950)

Foy Meets Girl (1950)

Studio Stoops (1950)

Brooklyn Buckaroos (1950)

Vagabond Loafers (1949)

Waiting in the Lurch (1949)

Fuelin' Around (1949)

Crime on Their Hands (1948)

(ELWOOD ULLMAN CONTINUED)

Mummy's Dummies (1948)

The Hot Scots (1948)

Flat Feat (1948)

Eight-Ball Andy (1948)

Shivering Sherlocks (1948)

Wedlock Deadlock (1947)

Wedding Belle (1947)

The Good Bad Egg (1947)

Susie Steps Out (1946)

Slappily Married (1946)

Men in Her Diary (1945)

Idiots Deluxe (1945)

Honeymoon Ahead (1945)

Open Season for Saps (1944)

Idle Roomers (1944)

The Kitchen Cynic (1944)

Mopey Dope (1944)

Busy Buddies (1944)

To Heir Is Human (1944)

Phony Express (1943)

Higher Than a Kite (1943)

Three Little Twirps (1943)

They Stooge to Conga (1943)

All Work and No Pay (1942)

Matri-Phony (1942)

Cactus Makes Perfect (1942)

Some More of Samoa (1941)

Love at First Fright (1941)

Dutiful But Dumb (1941)

So You Won't Squawk (1941)

Cold Turkey (1940)

No Census, No Feeling (1940)

The Spook Speaks (1940)

How High Is Up? (1940)

Boobs in the Woods (1940)

You're Next (1940)

A Plumbing We Will Go (1940)

Mr. Clyde Goes to Broadway (1940) w/Harry Edwards

His Bridal Fright (1940)

Teacher's Pest (1939)

Calling All Curs (1939)

Saved by the Belle (1939)

Yes, We Have No Bonanza (1939)

We Want Our Mummy (1939)

A Doggone Mixup (1938)

Mutts to You (1938)

The Nightshirt Bandit (1938)

Violent Is the Word for Curly (1938)

Tassels in the Air (1938)

Termites of 1938 (1938)

Gracie at the Bat (1937)

Playing the Ponies (1937)
    w/Al Giebler and Charlie Melson

Cash and Carry (1937) w/Clyde Bruckman

The Wrong Miss Wright (1937) w/Al Giebler

New News (1937) w/Al Giebler and Searle Kramer

The Hollywood Handicap (1932)

Hollywood Kids (1932) w/Ray Mayer

Foiled Again (1932)

GORE VIDAL (1925-)

Vidal is the Henry Adams of American letters, and the John Quincy Adams of American screenwriting. Scion, black sheep, and arguably the brightest bulb in an already incandescent political family, Gore, like Henry Adams, grew up to find himself constitutionally disqualified for the statesman's life he once seemed born to.

Not surprisingly, this tragic lack of what young Bill Clinton called "future political viability" plays out in Vidal's two best-known scripts. In *The Best Man*, adapted from his durably witty Broadway play, several candidates vie for their party's presidential nomination despite an assortment of private disqualifications, including one's homosexual past and, even worse, another's pesky conscience. And in *Ben-Hur* (for which Vidal self-reportedly wrote the first half, Christopher Fry wrote the second half, and Karl Tunberg got sole credit) the title character is a Jewish prince with every qualification it takes to lead Rome except what his boyhood friend Messina has: the right bloodline. Whether adapting his own play or Lew Wallace's biblical novel, Vidal makes the drama literally his own. He's also a first-rate craftsman who's written or doctored a raft of fine scripts and teleplays, but—as with the presidency of Henry Adams' grandfather, John Quincy, who was much better as a senator—this is hardly the greatest of his accomplishments.

To Forget Palermo (1990)

Billy the Kid (1989) (TV)

Lincoln (1988) (TV) (from his novel)

The Sicilian (1987) (uncredited)

Dress Gray (1986) (TV)

Caligula (1979)

Recht in eigen hand (1973) (TV)

Myra Breckinridge (1970)

Last of the Mobile Hot Shots (1970)

Is Paris Burning? (1966)

On the March to the Sea (1966) (TV)

The Best Man (1964) (from his play)

Visit to a Small Planet (1960) (from his play)

Suddenly, Last Summer (1959)

Ben-Hur (1959) (uncredited)

Startime (1959)

Sunday Showcase (1959)

The Scapegoat (1959) (adaptation)

The Left Handed Gun (1958) (from his play)

I Accuse! (1958)

The Catered Affair (1956)

Climax! (1954)

CALDER WILLINGHAM (1922-1995)

It's a shame Willingham is most often remembered for a movie he probably didn't write. Although he shares screen credit on *The Graduate* with Buck Henry, according to director Mike Nichols Willingham only wrote an early draft that Henry never read. We're free to take Nichols' account *cum grano salis*, but his contrasting graciousness about Henry's own contributions gives his recollection the ring of truth. "I took advantage of Buck to really figure out ways of shooting things," Nichols recalled to historian Joseph Gelmis in *The Film Director as Superstar*. "Like that whole montage out of the pool, into Mrs. Robinson's bed, ending up leaping out of the water, landing on Mrs. Robinson...Buck and I did together over days and days and days."

So if Willingham lucked into his half of *The Graduate*'s Writers Guild award and Oscar nomination via the WGA's baroque credit system, what distinctions *can* he claim? Plenty. Publishing generally well-received novels all the while, Willingham wrote or helped write some of modern Hollywood's best movies. If one wanted to take a Willingham title out of context as a template for his career, one could do worse than *The Strange One*, adapted from his book and play *End as a Man*. Willingham almost always turns his attention to the strange ones, the rebel outsiders, the iconoclastic outlaws who usually wind up martyred for their trouble. Think of the WWI soldiers shot by a firing squad to pay for their general's incompetence in *Paths of Glory*, the Thracian slaves who cry out, "I am Spartacus!" and end up crucified along with their leader, the persecuted Depression-era transgressors of *Thieves Like Us* and *Rambling Rose*. The odd film out here, and perhaps Willingham's strongest, may be his adaptation of Thomas Berger's novel *Little Big Man*. In that film, atypically for Willingham, the 112-year-old hero is consistently denied the surcease of martyrdom, only to watch it overtake almost everyone he loves. It's an irony Willingham—famous for a movie he didn't write, all but forgotten for his other, very real, attainments—might have appreciated.

Rambling Rose (1991) (from his novel)

Thou Shalt Not Commit Adultery (1978) (TV)
   w/Del Reisman

Thieves Like Us (1974)
   w/Joan Tewkesbury and Robert Altman

Little Big Man (1970)

The Graduate (1967) w/Buck Henry

One-Eyed Jacks (1961) w/Guy Trosper

Spartacus (1960)
   (uncredited battle scenes) w/Dalton Trumbo

The Vikings (1958) w/Dale Wasserman

Paths of Glory (1957)
   w/Stanley Kubrick and Jim Thompson

The Strange One (1957) (from his novel)

The Philco Television Playhouse (1948) TV Series

PHILIP YORDAN (1914–2003)

Before we conclude with the master cracksman, the screenwriter who finally solved Thomas Keneally's *Schindler's List* after a parade of suitors had already tried, we turn to Philip Yordan, the Oskar Schindler of the Blacklist. What Schindler was to Jewish factory workers in occupied Poland—if the analogy isn't too abhorrent—Yordan was to the blacklisted screenwriters around him in Paris and Spain. Ever the shadiest of businessmen, Yordan gave blacklistees work when no one else would, kept their identities from prying eyes, and made out like a bandit in the bargain. If Schindler was the archetypal "righteous gentile" among Jews, Yordan was, to ex-communists, the righteous capitalist. Almost certainly both a screenwriter himself and a front for other scribes, he might best be described with the same word Schindler's detractors have pinned on *him*: collaborationist.

Thomson includes Yordan in the *Biographical Dictionary of Film* as a "buoy to mark an area of whirlpool, crosscurrents, rocks, and wrecks." Patrick McGilligan, in the second of his three (and, one hopes, counting) *Backstory* volumes of interviews with screenwriters, calls Yordan "a chameleon," and includes not just a filmography but an "anti-filmography," ticking off arguments against Yordan's authorship on just about all his official screen credits. (Mercifully, the argument that he didn't direct any of them never comes up.) And the critic and eventual director Bertrand Tavernier admits of his 1962 *Cahiers du Cinema* interview with Yordan—the infrequent *Cahiers* interview with anyone other than a director—that "Yordan fooled me. He understood very quickly what I wanted to hear, and he said it."

To tease out the strains in a Yordan picture that are his own and not a collaborator's—or a subcontractor's—is a job worthy of Job. Adding to the obfuscation is the fact that many of Yordan's B pictures are impossible to find without recourse to a great video rental archive, like the sainted mail-order mavens at Eddie Brandt's Saturday Matinee in North Hollywood. But Thomson claims of Yordan that "it would be hard not to see a pattern of tough loners, dangerous situations, laconic women, and doomy finishes. In short, it sounds like movies."

Yordan himself sounds like a blackguard, a bullshit artist of the highest odor, and precisely the sort of larger-than-life figure that screenwriters could probably use more of, to set against the romantic genius-with-a-riding-crop archetype that directors have been disingenuously peddling for decades. The name of Yordan's own production company may tell us as much as we'll ever definitively learn about what drove this *polisheh* Chicago kid all the way from an Oscar nomination for *Dillinger* in 1945 to running a European screenwriting sweatshop in the '50s, to writing video quickies in his San Diego garage well into his seventies: Security Pictures.

Too Bad About Jack (1994)
Dead Girls Don't Tango (1992)
Marilyn Alive and Behind Bars (1992)
The Unholy (1988)

Cry Wilderness (1986)

Night Train to Terror (1985)

Bloody Wednesday (1985)

Death Wish Club (1983)

Cataclysm (1980)

Bad Man's River (1971) w/Eugenio Martin

Captain Apache (1971) w/Milton Sperling

The Royal Hunt of the Sun (1969)

Battle of the Bulge (1965)

    (front for Bernard Gordon)

    w/Milton Sperling and John Melson

Circus World (1964) (front for Bernard Gordon)

The Fall of the Roman Empire (1964) w/Ben Barzman

55 Days at Peking (1963)

    (uncredited w/Ben Barzman) w/ Bernard Gordon

The Day of the Triffids (1962) (front for Bernard Gordon)

El Cid (1961) w/Ben Barzman

King of Kings (1961)

Studs Lonigan (1960)

The Bramble Bush (1960) w/Milton Sperling

Day of the Outlaw (1959)

Anna Lucasta (1959) (from his play)

God's Little Acre (1958) (front for Ben Maddow)

The Fiend Who Walked the West (1958) w/Harry Brown

The Bravados (1958)

Island Woman (1958)

No Down Payment (1957) (front for Ben Maddow)

Street of Sinners (1957) (story)

Gun Glory (1957) (front for Ben Maddow)

Men in War (1957) (front for Ben Maddow)

Four Boys and a Gun (1957)

The Harder They Fall (1956)

The Last Frontier (1955) w/Russell S. Hughes

The Man from Laramie (1955) w/Frank Burt

Conquest of Space (1955) (adaptation)

The Big Combo (1955)

Joe MacBeth (1955)

Broken Lance (1954) (story)

Johnny Guitar (1954)

The Naked Jungle (1954)
    (front for Ben Maddow) w/Ranald Macdougall

Man Crazy (1953)

Blowing Wild (1953) (also story)

Houdini (1953)

Mara Maru (1952)
    w/Sidney Harmon, Hollister Noble, and N. Richard Nash

Mutiny (1952)

Detective Story (1951) w/Robert Wyler

Drums in the Deep South (1951)

Edge of Doom (1950)

Reign of Terror (1949) w/Aeneas MacKenzie

Anna Lucasta (1949) (also play)

House of Strangers (1949)

Bad Men of Tombstone (1949) w/Arthur Strawn

The Chase (1946)

Suspense (1946)

Whistle Stop (1946)

Dillinger (1945)

When Strangers Marry (1944) w/Dennis Cooper

Johnny Doesn't Live Here Any More (1944)

The Unknown Guest (1943)

Syncopation (1942) w/Frank Cavett and Valentine Davies

STEVEN ZAILLIAN (1953-)

In addition to working through his youthful alienation and parental anxiety in a couple of fascinating films (*The Falcon and the Snowman*, *Searching for Bobby Fischer*), Zaillian has to his credit one of the most ingenious screenwriting solutions of recent decades. The picture was *Schindler's List*. The problem? Oskar Schindler saved more than 1,000 Jews from Auschwitz, and then…nothing. His postwar biography dissipates into 30 years of penury and alcoholism. If this were fiction, Schindler would surely have martyred himself for "his" Jews and become a secular saint for his sacrifice. Instead he overstayed his welcome, acting like a man more tormented by conscience than subservient to it. How on earth do you dramatize that? Zaillian cracks the problem in just five words: "I could have done more."

You remember. Schindler stands before his assembled workers, gathered in one of Spielberg's signature curtain-call finales. (Remember the mothership's farewell to the scientists at the end of *Close Encounters*? The miracle of the ark in front of the Nazis, in the natural amphitheatre at the end of *Raiders*? E.T.'s valediction to Elliott before their wonderstruck pursuers at the end of that picture? In each case, this "born moviemaker" blocked out a scene so theatrical, the only thing missing is a follow-spot and a proscenium arch. Just because screenwriters have thematic signatures, as I've endeavored to prove, doesn't mean that directors don't.)

So Schindler's addressing the Jews he saved, and what does he say? "I could have done more. I should have sold this car. It would have been 10 more if I sold this car. This pen, it would have been five more...This ring, the gold in this ring, I could have gotten two...."

It's a great scene, but why? Because it presents a viable solution to the enigma of Schindler's postwar collapse: He never forgave himself for the lives he *didn't* save. Even more important, it throws the moral question of the movie right into the audience's lap. If Schindler himself, the great savior, could have done more, what's our excuse? How many cars do we need? How many pens, how many rings, how many stupid trinkets have we bought while people are dying for a lousy drink of water? It's a great scene precisely because it refuses to let the viewer off the hook. As in Zaillian's other movies about the nature of evil, the challenge suddenly becomes not "What would we have done in the hero's place?" but "What would a hero do in ours?"

All the King's Men (2005)
The Interpreter (2005)
    w/Charles Randolph, Scott Frank,
    Martin Stellman, and Brian Ward
Gangs of New York (2002)
    w/Jay Cocks and Kenneth Lonergan
Hannibal (2001)
    w/David Mamet and Thomas Harris
A Civil Action (1998)
Mission: Impossible (1996)
    w/Robert Towne and David Koepp
Clear and Present Danger (1994)
    w/Donald Stewart and John Milius
Schindler's List (1993)
Searching for Bobby Fischer (1993)
Jack the Bear (1993)
Awakenings (1990)
The Falcon and the Snowman (1985)

POST-CREDIT
SEQUENCE

I.

There, that drove a nice stake through the heart of *auteurism*, didn't it? No?

No. Of course not. What we have here is at best a hasty prolegomenon to any further screenwriter-centered film criticism, hamstrung by what looks like a partiality to white males surpassing even that of the major studios—whose output the list disproportionately favors. The thumbnail entries accompanying the credits pretty much ignore source material, collaborators, and dozens of films that don't fit the writers' purported signatures nearly as well as those that do. These thumbnails also downplay most of the screenwriters' bad movies, and totally discount the very real possibility that writers' distinctive themes have emerged, not because they reflect these scribblers' inmost obsessions, but rather because their employers typecast them and wouldn't let them do much else.

Now, what dubious school of film criticism does this remind us of? Hands?

You get the point. But director-centric and writer-centric film criticism are far from equally worthless. For a final idea of why, it may help to take a brief look at *auteurism's* secret idiot brother: management consulting.

Along about mid-century, America's managers looked around and noticed that their employees were doing all the work, while they themselves had to make do with getting rich. All they had to show for everybody else's elbow grease was money and guilt. To massage their money, they devised tax shelters; to massage their guilt, an entire pseudo-science grew up around motivating other people— many of whom were already fully motivated by pride, or by the need to feed their families. Thus was the myth of the master manager born.

The parallel to film directing isn't exactly opaque here. Almost every member of the film-making team—from the writer to the author of the source material, to the actors, to the director of photography, to the gaffer—almost everyone has a story about seeing his own work attributed to someone else, usually the director, in a review.

Perhaps only the director has no experience of this. It's the classic worker's complaint: I did all this work, and my boss took the credit. Directors and managers alike live in fear of hearing one question: "Yes, but what exactly do you *do*?" So much so, in fact, that they've devised two separate answers for it. The public answer is, more or less, "Delegate." The private answer is, of course, "Everything."

This book began with a paraphrase of E.M. Forster to the effect that film is, "yes—oh, dear, yes"—a collaborative art. The *schreiber* theory should in no way be construed as a disavowal of this inescapable axiom. Screenwriters don't do it all, any more than directors do—or maybe a little more than directors do, at least on the best movies. *Schreiberism* is, among other things, an attempt to rescue reviewing and scholarship from those who would have us forget just how collaborative filmmaking truly is. If the idea of finding recurrent patterns and themes in anyone but a director's work seems heretical today, chalk it up to *auteurism's* fifty-year head start.

Finally, before the lights come up, it may help to think of film history as a ketch under sail. Fifty years ago, well-meaning *auteur* theorists grabbed the tiller and steered us away from shoals of producer and studio worship. Nowadays, just about everybody thinking about movies is arrayed on the director's side of the boat. Not coincidentally, film criticism, and arguably American film itself, stand in danger of capsizing under the weight of all that unanimity. If we're ever to tack back toward the true horizon, a course correction will be needed—maybe even the over-correction charted in this book. To be sure, *schreiberism* is bound to strike some film buffs as a waterspout well worth avoiding. But is anybody genuinely excited about where American movies are headed without it?

II.

The ability of artists to change the climate surrounding art—and of criticism to change the very climate around us—has never been more perfectly expressed than by Oscar Wilde in *The Decay of Lying*. In that famous dialogue, two aesthetes names Vivian and Cyril discuss the strangely reciprocal realms of art and life. At one point, Vivian remarks that, "The extraordinary change that has taken place in the climate of London during the last ten years is entirely due to a particular school of Art."

Whether from assent or astonishment, Cyril makes no response to this, and Vivian quickly proceeds to his paradoxical conclusion: "At present, people see fogs, not because there are fogs, but because poets and painters have taught them the mysterious loveliness of such effects. There may have been fogs for centuries in London. I dare say there were. But no one saw them, and so we do not know anything about them. They did not exist until Art had invented them."

Just as nobody noticed London fogs until painters pointed them out by painting them, I'd contend that most screenwriters have gone disproportionately unnoticed for the simple reason that no disinterested party has bothered to state (or overstate) the case for their centrality. So far as most critics are concerned, screenwriters, like London fogs before painters discovered them, do not exist. To a lesser extent, this was true of directors before the coming of *auteurism*, and has been true of producers ever since.

Seen in this light, alas, a movie's true author isn't the director, the producer, or anybody else on the payroll, even the screenwriter. No, the true author of any film—the only one with the power to fix its image in the public mind, and to determine its lasting worth—remains the critic.